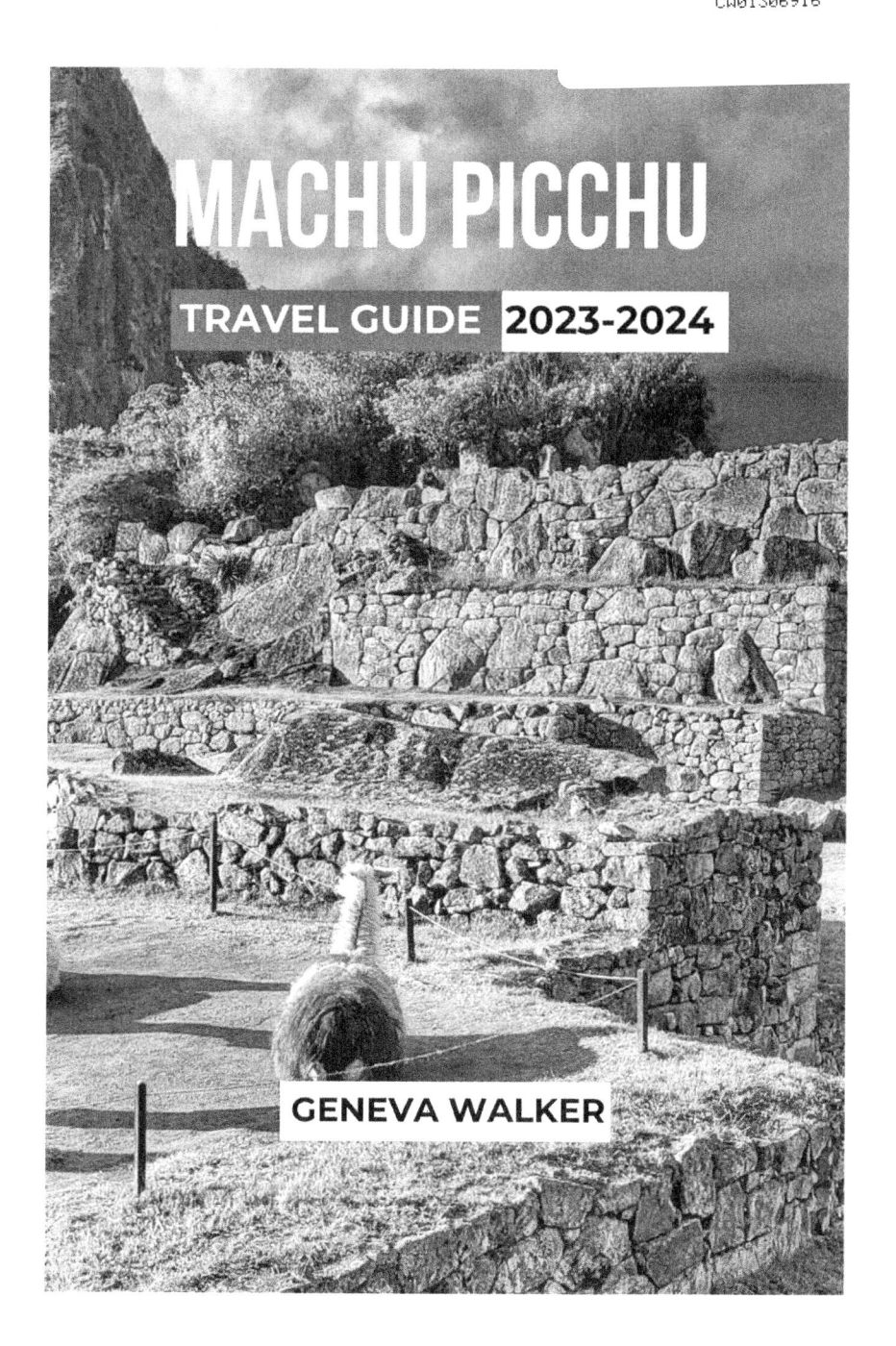

MACHU PICCHU

TRAVEL GUIDE 2023-2024

GENEVA WALKER

MACHU PICCHU TRAVEL GUIDE 2023-2024

The Ultimate Guide to Discovering Top Attractions, Activities, where to stay and what to Eat in Machu Picchu.

All rights reserved. No part of this publication may be reproduced, distributed, or transmitted in any form or by any means, including
photocopying, recording, or other electronic or mechanical methods, without the prior written permission of the publisher, except in the case of brief quotations embodied in critical reviews and certain other noncommercial uses permitted by copyright law.

Copyright © Geneva Walker, 2023.

Table of Contents

INTRODUCTION 8

    MY MEMORABLE EXPERIENCE 8

    WHY VISIT MACHU PICCHU? 13

    HISTORY AND MYSTERY OF THE INCA CITY 16

    HOW TO VISIT MACHU PICCHU 21

    HOW TO PLAN YOUR TRIP 24

        When to go 24

        How to get there 25

        Where to stay 26

        What to see 27

        How to avoid the crowd 29

CHAPTER 1 34

    GETTING TO MACHU PICCHU 34

    TREK: CHOICES, DIFFICULTY, AND PERMITS 44

    BY CAR: BENEFITS AND DRAWBACKS OF DRIVING TO MACHU PICCHU 50

CHAPTER 2 58

Exploring Machu Picchu 58
What to see and do at the Citadel of Machu Picchu 60
How to join a tour 72
How to escape the crowds and enjoy the scenery 78

CHAPTER 3 82

Staying near Machu Picchu 82
Aguas Calientes: hotels, restaurants, and hot springs . 83
Camping: where to pitch your tent and what to bring .. 89
Where to camp near Machu Picchu 89
Luxury options 97

CHAPTER 4 100

Beyond Machu Picchu 100
Huayna Picchu: how to climb the legendary peak 102
Machu Picchu Mountain: an alternate walk with spectacular vistas 106

THE SUN GATE AND THE INCA BRIDGE: SIMPLE TREKS WITH HISTORICAL IMPORTANCE 110

CHAPTER 5 114

CUSCO AND THE SACRED VALLEY 114

CUSCO: THE HISTORIC CAPITAL OF THE INCA EMPIRE AND A UNESCO WORLD HERITAGE SITE 116

OLLANTAYTAMBO: A PICTURESQUE VILLAGE WITH SPECTACULAR RUINS AND A RAILROAD STATION 124

PISAC: A VIBRANT MARKET AND A HIGH FORTIFICATION 132

CHAPTER 6 138

3-6 DAYS ITINERARY FOR MACHU PICCHU 138

Day 1: Arrival in Cusco 138

Day 2: Sacred Valley Tour 141

Day 4: Transfer to Cusco 147

Day 5: Cusco Free Day 148

Day 6: Departure from Cusco 149

CHAPTER 7: TRAVEL TIPS 154

WHEN IS THE IDEAL TIME TO VISIT MACHU PICCHU? 154

WHAT TO TAKE FOR YOUR VACATION TO MACHU PICCHU 159

HOW TO ACQUIRE YOUR MACHU PICCHU ADMISSION TICKET?165

HOW TO BE A CAREFUL TRAVELER? 170

VISA REQUIREMENTS FOR MACHU PICCHU 175

CUSTOM AND ETIQUETTE 183

LANGUAGE AND COMMUNICATION 187

HEALTH AND SAFETY ADVICE 191

IMPORTANT PHRASES TO KNOW 197

CONCLUSION 204

INTRODUCTION

My Memorable Experience

I was captivated by the old fascinating city, buried in the sky, and wondered what mysteries it contained. I eventually had the opportunity to visit Machu Picchu in 2023 with my closest friend. It was one of the most amazing journeys of my life, and I want to share it with you how we made it happen, what we saw and did, and how the locals welcomed us.

How We Traveled to Machu Picchu

The settlement at the base of Machu Picchu, Aguas Calientes, is where we decided to go by train from Cusco. We purchased our tickets online via PeruRail, which provides numerous alternatives based on your budget and desire. We picked the Vistadome service, which has panoramic windows and a glass ceiling that enable you to experience wonderful views along the journey. The train travel took around 3.5 hours, and live music, refreshments, and beverages entertained us.

We arrived in Aguas Calientes about midday and checked into our hotel, the Inkaterra Machu Picchu Pueblo Hotel, a luxury eco-lodge surrounded by beautiful gardens and hummingbirds. We grabbed lunch at their restaurant, which provides great Peruvian cuisine with organic products from their farm. We particularly appreciated their spa, which includes massages, a sauna, and hot springs.

The following morning, we rose early to board the first bus to Machu Picchu. We booked our admission tickets online via the official website, which is highly advised since they sell out rapidly. We also hired a tour via our hotel, who greeted us at the bus terminal and escorted us during our vacation. He was extremely informed and polite and explained to us the place's history, culture, and architecture.

Exploring Machu Picchu

We entered Machu Picchu via the Sun Gate, where the Inca Trail terminates. We were welcomed by a beautiful panorama of the citadel, with the Huayna Picchu mountain rising behind it. We snapped some shots and followed our guide to visit the various areas of the city.

We visited the Temple of the Sun, where the Incas worshipped their major deity; the Intihuatana stone, where they timed the seasons; the Royal Tomb, where they buried their nobility; the Sacred Plaza, where they performed festivities; and many more. We also strolled down the agricultural terraces utilized for cultivation and irrigation. We learned how the Incas created this remarkable metropolis using perfect engineering and astronomical abilities without using mortar or wheels.

We spent around four hours in Machu Picchu and then chose to climb Huayna Picchu for an added challenge. This climb required a separate ticket, which we had also acquired in advance. It was a steep and narrow path, with some portions needing ropes and ladders. It took us about an hour to reach the top, but it was worth it. The view from there was incredible: we could see the entire city below us and the neighboring mountains and valleys. We felt like we were on top of the world.

Welcome by the Locals

One of the finest elements of our vacation was meeting and connecting with the locals. They were incredibly kind, accommodating, and always eager to assist us with everything we needed. They also shared their culture and customs with us, which helped us respect their way of life.

We met several local artists in Aguas Calientes who offered us lovely products made of alpaca wool, silver, wood, and stone. They also showed us how to manufacture some of them, such as bracelets and earrings. We also met several local musicians at our hotel who performed traditional instruments such as flutes, drums, and charangos. They sang songs in Quechua, the language of the Incas, and urged us to join them.

We also met several local farmers in Cusco, who asked us to tour their fields and learn about their crops. They showed us how they cultivate potatoes, maize, quinoa, coca leaves, and other natural plants. They also explained how they utilize them for food, medicine, and ceremonies. They also prepared a classic cuisine called pachamanca, consisting of meat and vegetables cooked underground using hot stones.

Why This Travel Guide Will Help You

This travel guide will assist you in thoroughly planning your vacation, with recommendations on how to get there, where to stay, what to see and do, and more. It will also offer you the latest information on health and safety precautions, admission criteria, the environmental rules to maintain this World Heritage Site, and much more.

Machu Picchu is a wonderful destination that will leave you in amazement and wonder. It is a once-in-a-lifetime chance that you don't want to miss. So book your tickets today, pack your luggage, and prepare for an incredible vacation. Machu Picchu awaits you!

Why visit Machu Picchu?

Machu Picchu is more than simply a tourist site. It is a place of wonder, intrigue, and inspiration. It is a tribute to the creativity and durability of the Inca civilization and a reminder of the beauty and variety of Peru. Here are some of the reasons why you should visit Machu Picchu in 2023-2024:

Discover the Incas' history and culture. Pachacuti, the Inca emperor, built Machu Picchu in the 15th century as a royal estate and a place of worship. It highlights the great accomplishments of the Inca people in construction, engineering, astronomy, and agriculture. You can visit the complex of temples, palaces, terraces, and fountains that depict the Inca cosmology and worldview. You can learn about the Inca culture and civilization from the local guides and specialists who will join you on your trip.

Enjoy the beautiful beauty and fauna of the Andes. Machu Picchu is in a magnificent environment, surrounded by lush mountains and valleys. The position provides:
- Amazing views of the Urubamba River.
- The snow-capped peaks of Salkantay and Veronica.

- The cloud forest blankets the slopes.

The region is home to diverse flora and animals, including orchids, hummingbirds, bears, and condors. You can immerse yourself in this unique habitat's natural beauty and richness.

Challenge yourself with an ambitious walk or excursion. Machu Picchu can be reached by rail or bus from Cusco, but if you are seeking a more adventurous way to get there, you can choose one of the numerous hiking or trekking alternatives available. The most renowned one is the Inca Trail, a four-day journey following the historical way the Incas traveled to reach Machu Picchu. The path travels through spectacular scenery, ancient sites, and high passes. Other possibilities are the Salkantay Trek, which covers a spectacular mountain range; the Lares Trek, which travels through traditional Andean towns; and the Short Inca Trail, perfect for individuals with limited time or physical endurance.

Discover further sights and activities in Peru. Machu Picchu is one of many attractions that Peru has to offer. You can visit intriguing sites and enjoy engaging activities in this varied country. For example, You can tour Cusco, a UNESCO World Heritage Site and the historic capital of the Inca Empire; visit the Sacred Valley, where you can see impressive Inca ruins and colorful markets; travel to Lake Titicaca, the world's highest navigable lake and the location of native communities; or venture into the Amazon rainforest, where you can encounter exotic wildlife and learn about indigenous cultures.

Machu Picchu is a place that will leave you stunned, and inspired. It is a spot that you will never forget. You should visit this destination at least once in your lifetime.

History and mystery of the Inca city

Machu Picchu, the "Old Peak" in Quechua, is a beautiful fortress of stone sitting on a rocky ridge above the Urubamba River valley in Peru. It was erected by the Inca Empire, who controlled a huge expanse of western South America from the 15th to the 16th century. But why was it built? Who resided there? And how did it stay concealed from the Spanish conquerors for centuries? These questions have captivated explorers, archaeologists, and visitors ever since its discovery in 1911 by Hiram Bingham, a Yale professor who was hunting for another lost city of the Incas.

The Inca Empire

The Inca Empire was pre-Columbian America's greatest and most sophisticated civilizations. It spanned from Colombia to Chile, embracing varied cultures, languages, and landscapes. The Incas were brilliant engineers, builders, farmers, and administrators who constructed remarkable roads, bridges, terraces, and fortresses across their empire. They built a sophisticated system of religion, governance, and social structure, based on worshiping the sun deity Inti and the divine authority of the Sapa Inca, or emperor.

The Inca Empire reached its height of growth and wealth under Pachacuti Inca Yupanqui (reigned 1438–71) and his son Topa Inca Yupanqui (reigned 1471–93), who conquered numerous surrounding peoples and areas. They launched the building of Machu Picchu, perhaps as a royal estate and ceremonial center for Pachacuti. However, the dominion soon faced internal unrest and external challenges from competing clans and illnesses introduced by European explorers.

The kingdom disintegrated following a civil war between two brothers, Huascar and Atahualpa, who claimed the throne after their father's death in 1525. Atahualpa conquered Huascar in 1532 but was arrested and murdered by Francisco Pizarro, the commander of a Spanish expedition that intended to take Peru. The Spanish invasion signaled the end of the Inca Empire and the beginning of a new colonial age.

The discovery of Machu Picchu

Machu Picchu was one of the few great Inca ruins that avoided destruction by the Spanish, presumably because of its remote and inaccessible position. The location was known exclusively to local farmers and peasants until 1911 when Hiram Bingham accidentally into it with the aid of a local child called Pablito Alvarez. Bingham was enthralled by the remains and felt he had reached Vilcabamba, the final sanctuary of the Incas, where they defied Spanish power until 1572. He published his discoveries in National Geographic magazine in 1913, bringing Machu Picchu to the world's attention1. He again went to Machu Picchu in 1912 and 1915 with the sponsorship of Yale University and the National Geographic Society to undertake more excavations and gather artifacts.

However, Bingham's identification of Machu Picchu as Vilcabamba was subsequently contested by other historians and explorers, who suggested that Vilcabamba was situated at another site named Espiritu Pampa, found by Bingham in 1911 but studied by Gene Savoy in 1964.

Machu Picchu's ultimate purpose and importance remain a mystery today, while various ideas have been offered. Some say that Machu Picchu was a holy city devoted to Inti or a pilgrimage destination for the Inca elite. Others suggest that Machu Picchu was a military fortification or an agricultural experiment site. Still, others argue that Machu Picchu was a hidden hideaway for the Sapa Inca or a symbolic portrayal of the Inca cosmos.

The enigma of Machu Picchu

Machu Picchu is not just a historical riddle but an architectural wonder. The complex consists of more than 200 structures separated into two major sectors: an urban sector with temples, palaces, residences, and plazas; and an agricultural sector with terraces, storehouses, and irrigation systems. The structures are composed of precisely cut stones that fit together without cement, producing earthquake-resistant and visually beautiful walls. The stones were mined from adjacent mountains and transported by human labor or llamas. The builders employed natural elements like caverns, rocks, and waterfalls to improve their architecture.

Machu Picchu exhibits the Inca's excellent grasp of astronomy, mathematics, and engineering. The location is aligned with the cardinal directions and the motions of the sun, moon, and stars. The Intihuatana, known as the "hitching post of the sun," is a carved stone that serves as a solar calendar and a reminder of the winter solstice. The Temple of the Sun, or Torreon, is a semicircular edifice that encloses a rock that casts a shadow on a stone altar at the summer solstice. The Temple of the Three Windows, or Qhapaq Kancha, is a rectangular tower with three trapezoidal windows that surround the mountains and represent the three worlds of the Inca cosmology:

- The higher world of the gods
- The middle world of the people
- The lower world of the dead

Machu Picchu is a tribute to the Inca's accomplishments and a source of inspiration and awe for millions of tourists who come to appreciate its beauty and mystery. Since 1983, the UNESCO has designated Machu Picchu as a World Heritage site, and in 2007, it was regarded as one of the New Seven Wonders of the World. It is a spiritual spot for many Peruvians who consider it a representation of their cultural identity and history. Machu Picchu is a location where history and mystery meet, nature and culture merge, and the past and present coexist.

How to visit Machu Picchu

About 50 miles (80 km) northwest of Cusco, the historic capital of the Inca Empire and a popular tourist destination in Peru, is where you'll find Machu Picchu. There are various routes to Machu Picchu from Cusco, depending on your price, time, and desire. The most common and easiest route is to take a train from Cusco to Aguas Calientes, the closest town to Machu Picchu, and then take a bus or climb to the monument. The train excursion takes around four hours and provides stunning vistas of the Urubamba River basin. Several kinds of trains are available, from luxury to economical, operated by PeruRail or IncaRail.

Another way to see Machu Picchu is to travel along the Inca Trail, a network of ancient routes linking numerous Inca monuments. The typical Inca Trail is a four-day walk that spans roughly 26 miles (42 km) and reaches a height of 13,800 feet (4,200 meters) at its highest point. The path travels across varied environments, such as cloud forests, alpine meadows, and ancient remains. The climax of the trek is arriving at Machu Picchu via the Sun Gate, or Intipunku, at daybreak on the fourth day. The Inca Trail is a tough yet rewarding trip requiring strong physical conditions, suitable equipment, and early booking.

There are several alternate pathways to Machu Picchu that provide varied degrees of effort and time. Some of them include the Salkantay Trail, which traverses a high mountain peak and takes five days; the Lares Trail, which travels through rural settlements and hot springs and takes four days; and the Choquequirao Trail, which leads to another remarkable Inca monument and takes eight days. Whichever path you select, you will need a qualified guide and a permit to access Machu Picchu.

Machu Picchu is accessible every day from 6 am until 5:30 pm. Two admission tickets are available: one that enables access to Machu Picchu just, and another that includes access to Huayna Picchu or Machu Picchu Mountain. These two peaks give panoramic views of the monument. The tickets have varying time slots and pricing based on the season and demand. You can purchase your tickets online or at authorized Cusco or Aguas Calientes offices.

Machu Picchu is a site that you will always remember once you see it. It is a location where you can learn about the history and mystery of the Inca civilization, admire their architectural and creative abilities, enjoys their harmony with nature, and sense their spiritual energy. It is a site that will make you wonder how they created it, why they built it, and what mysteries it still bears. This spot will encourage you to discover more of Peru's rich culture and landscapes.

How to Plan your Trip

Machu Picchu is one of the world's most renowned and awe-inspiring sites, but organizing a trip there can be stressful. There are numerous aspects to consider, such as when to travel, how to get there, where to stay, what to see, and how to escape the crowds. We have created this guide with valuable ideas and suggestions to help you make the most of your stay.

When to go

The optimal time to visit Machu Picchu depends on your interests and priorities. The main season is from June through August when the weather is dry and bright but chilly and crowded. This is the season when the Inca Trail is open and most popular, so you must reserve well in advance to trek it. The low season is from December through February when the weather is damp and overcast but milder and less crowded. This is the season when the Inca Trail is closed for repair, but you can still approach Machu Picchu by train or alternate hikes. The off-peak months are March through Can and September through November, when the weather is more varied and unpredictable but pleasant and less crowded. These are the greatest times to observe the flora and fauna in bloom.

How to get there

The simplest and quickest method to go to Machu Picchu is by rail from Cusco or Ollantaytambo. Various train companies provide varying services and comfort, such as PeruRail, IncaRail, or MachuPicchu Train. The train ride takes around 3.5 hours from Cusco or 1.5 hours from Ollantaytambo and concludes at Aguas Calientes, the village at the foot of Machu Picchu. You must take a bus or trek for around 30 minutes to reach the site entrance.

The most exciting and gratifying way to travel to Machu Picchu is by trekking one of the several paths there. The most renowned and demanding one is the Inca Trail, a four-day hike that follows the historical path of the Incas through breathtaking landscapes and archaeological sites. The Inca Trail has a restricted capacity of 500 people per day, including guides and porters, so you need to book months in advance via a certified tour operator. The Inca Trail is closed in February for repairs.

Other alternate treks give distinct sensations and viewpoints of Machu Picchu, such as the Salkantay Trek, the Lares Trek, or the Choquequirao Trek7. These treks vary in duration, complexity, and expense, but they all demand a fair degree of fitness and planning. They finish at Aguas Calientes, where you need to take a bus or climb to reach Machu Picchu.

Where to stay

Most tourists stay at Aguas Calientes, the village near Machu Picchu. There are many housing alternatives, ranging from inexpensive hostels to luxury hotels. Some of the greatest include Sumaq Hotel, Inkaterra Machu Picchu Pueblo Hotel, and El MaPi by Inkaterra. Aguas Calientes offers restaurants, shops, marketplaces, and hot springs to enjoy after a long day of touring.

The only hotel inside Machu Picchu is Belmond Sanctuary Lodge, which provides unrivaled views and access to the monument. However, it is highly pricey and typically completely booked. If you wish to stay there, you need to book well in advance and be prepared to pay a premium fee.

What to see

Machu Picchu is a big and complicated site that occupies an area of nearly 5 square kilometers. It comprises more than 200 buildings and constructions that serve varied functions, such as temples, palaces, residences, warehouses, terraces, fountains, and observatories. The site is split into two primary sectors: the urban sector and the agricultural sector.

- The urban sector is where most of the significant buildings are situated, such as:

- The Temple of the Sun is a semicircular edifice that coincides with the solstices and holds a carved stone used as an altar or sundial.

- The Intihuatana: a sculpted stone that resembles a hitching post for the sun. It was utilized as an astronomy tool and a holy emblem of the Inca worldview.

- The Temple of the Three Windows: a rectangular tower with three trapezoidal windows facing east and framing the mountains. It was devoted to the three worlds of the Inca civilization: Hanan Pacha (the top world), Kay Pacha (the middle world), and Uku Pacha (the bottom world).

- The Principal Temple: a massive tower that has three walls and a central altar. It was utilized for religious rites and rituals.

- The Temple of the Condor: a building that mimics the form of a condor, a holy animal for the Incas. It has a sculpted stone that portrays the head and wings of the condor and a natural rock that symbolizes its torso and feet.

- The Royal Tomb is a cave-like building with a carved stone used as a sarcophagus or altar. It is encircled by niches that hold mummies and offerings.

- The agricultural sector is where most of the terraces and warehouses are situated, such as:

1. The Agricultural Terraces: a set of platforms utilized for cultivation and irrigation. They acted as an erosion control device and a landscape design feature.

2. The Guardhouse: a tiny building that overlooks the place and the valley. It was utilized as an observation point and a checkpoint for tourists.

3. The Funerary Rock: a big carved stone that was utilized as a location for mummification and burial. It is positioned near the property's entrance and gives a panoramic view.

How to avoid the crowd

Machu Picchu is one of the most visited locations in the world, receiving more than 1.5 million tourists every year. It can become busy and raucous, particularly during peak seasons and hours. To escape the crowds and have a more tranquil and genuine experience, you might follow these tips:

Reserve your tickets in advance: Machu Picchu has a restricted capacity of 2,500 people daily. Therefore, you must immediately reserve your tickets online or via an authorized agency. You need to pick between two-time slots: morning (6 am to 12 pm) or afternoon (12 pm to 5:30 pm). You can only access the site once per ticket, so plan your visit appropriately.

Hire a guide: Machu Picchu is a magnificent location and a historical and cultural value. To truly grasp its importance and mysteries, you must hire a guide to explain its history, architecture, and symbolism. You can hire a guide at the entrance to the site or via your hotel or tour operator. A guided tour normally lasts approximately 2 hours and costs roughly 20 USD per person.

Explore beyond the major attractions: Machu Picchu has more to offer than only the urban section and the agriculture sector. You can visit other sites and perspectives that are less busy and more picturesque, such as:

The Sun Gate: a stone gate that marks the end of the Inca Trail and gives a spectacular view of Machu Picchu from above. It takes around an hour to trek there from the location.

The Inca Bridge: a wooden bridge that traverses a tight opening on the side of the mountain. It was part of an alternate path to Machu Picchu employed for security considerations. It takes roughly 20 minutes to walk there from the site.

Huayna Picchu: a high mountain that rises above Machu Picchu and gives a beautiful view of the ruins and the valley. It takes around an hour to climb from the site, but you need to obtain a separate ticket in advance since only 400 people are permitted daily.

Machu Picchu Mountain is another mountain that overlooks Machu Picchu and gives a panoramic view. It takes roughly 2 hours to trek there from the site, but you must obtain a separate ticket in advance since only 800 people are permitted daily.

Planning a vacation to Machu Picchu needs some study and planning, but it is well worth the effort. Machu Picchu is a unique and breathtaking destination that will leave you astonished and impressed. Whether you ride the train or trek the route, you will have a memorable journey and a lifelong memory. Machu Picchu is more than simply a tourist attraction; it is a cultural and historical treasure that demands your attention and appreciation.

CHAPTER 1

Getting to Machu Picchu

Machu Picchu is much more than simply a tourist destination. It is a holy location that unveils the secrets of a vanished civilization. It is a masterwork of engineering and construction that defies the laws of nature. It is a cultural gem that exhibits the variety and depth of the Andean world. It is a marvel that provokes astonishment, curiosity, and adoration.

Machu Picchu is one of the world's most recognized and visited sites, drawing millions of people every year. This ancient Inca fortress, situated in the high Andes of Peru, is a UNESCO World Heritage Site and one of the World's New Seven Wonders. It is a masterpiece of engineering, architecture, and culture and a tribute to the accomplishments of the Inca civilization.

But how can you go to this beautiful place? How do you uncover its secret nooks and mysteries? How can you make the most of your once-in-a-lifetime experience? In this chapter, we will guide you through navigating Machu

Picchu, from picking the best approach to getting there to finding its key attractions and features. We will provide you with some tips and methods on how to enjoy your vacation safely, ethically, and politely.

By train: routes, pricing, and timetables

One of the most popular and easiest methods to visit Machu Picchu, the ancient Inca fortress and one of the Seven Wonders of the World, is by train. The train ride provides breathtaking views of the Andean terrain and pleasant and diverse services to suit various budgets and interests. Two railway companies run the Cusco – Machu Picchu route: Peru Rail and Inca Rail. Both businesses provide comparable routes and timetables but vary in the sorts of services and rates they offer. Here is a guide to help you pick the best train choice for your Machu Picchu excursion.

Peru Rail

Peru Rail is the main train company and railway operator in southern Peru for freight and passengers. It has many routes, but the main one is Poroy - Ollantaytambo - Aguas Calientes (Machu Picchu Pueblo). It will have a new route beginning in 2019: San Pedro (in Cusco) - Poroy -

Ollantaytambo - Aguas Calientes. Peru Rail operates four kinds of train services to Machu Picchu for international visitors (Expedition, Vistadome, Hiram Bingham, and Sacred Valley) and one local train service for Peruvians and foreign residents.

Expedition

The Expedition service is Peru Rail's cheapest and most basic option. It offers comfy seats, panoramic windows, baggage racks, air conditioning, heating, and onboard food and refreshments for sale. The Expedition service begins at Poroy station (about 30 minutes from Cusco by taxi) or Ollantaytambo station (about 2 hours from Cusco by bus or taxi). It arrives at Aguas Calientes station (the closest town to Machu Picchu). The travel time ranges from 1 hour 45 minutes to 3 hours 30 minutes, depending on the departure station. A one-way trip costs vary from $65 to $85 per person.

Vistadome

The Vistadome service is more elegant and comfortable than the Expedition service. It boasts roomy seats, panoramic windows on the top and the sides, baggage racks, air conditioning, heating, and onboard refreshments and beverages included in the ticket price. The Vistadome service includes cultural entertainment, such as live music and dancing throughout the voyage. The Vistadome service leaves from Poroy station or Ollantaytambo station and arrives at Aguas Calientes station. The travel time ranges from 1 hour 30 minutes to 3 hours 15 minutes, depending on the departure station. The costs vary from $85 USD to $105 USD per person for a one-way trip.

Hiram Bingham

The Hiram Bingham service is Peru Rail's most premium and luxurious option. It is named after the American adventurer who found Machu Picchu in 1911. It boasts magnificent cars furnished like the 1920s Pullman trains, with leather couches, polished wood, brass fixtures, and huge windows. The Hiram Bingham service includes gourmet dinners, excellent wines, beverages, live music, guided tours, and admission tickets to Machu Picchu in the ticket fee. The Hiram Bingham service leaves Poroy station and arrives at Aguas Calientes station. The trip duration is 3 hours and 15 minutes. For a one-way trip, the rates vary from $480 to $550 per person.

Sacred Valley

The Sacred Valley service is a new option provided by Peru Rail starting in 2019. It is meant for those who wish to experience the Sacred Valley of the Incas before visiting Machu Picchu. It includes contemporary carriages with panoramic windows, comfy seats, baggage racks, air conditioning, heating, and onboard refreshments and beverages included in the ticket price. The Sacred Valley service leaves at San Pedro station (in the city of Cusco) or Urubamba station (in the center of the Sacred Valley) and arrives at Aguas Calientes station. The travel duration ranges from 3 hours to 4 hours, depending on the departure location. A one-way trip costs vary from $120 to $140 per person.

Inca Rail

Inca Rail is another railway company that runs the Cusco – Machu Picchu route. It provides three kinds of train services to Machu Picchu for international visitors (The Voyager, The 360°, and The First Class) and one local train service just for Peruvians and foreign inhabitants.

The Voyager

The Voyager service is the cheapest and most basic option Inca Rail provides. It offers comfy seats, panoramic windows, baggage racks, air conditioning, heating, and onboard food and refreshments for sale. The Voyager service leaves from Ollantaytambo station and arrives at Aguas Calientes station. The trip time is 1 hour 45 minutes. The costs vary from $65 USD to $75 USD per person for a one-way trip.

The 360°

The 360° service is more luxurious and pleasant than the Voyager service. It boasts roomy seats, panoramic windows on the top and the sides, baggage racks, air conditioning, heating, and onboard refreshments and beverages included in the ticket price. The 360° service provides an observation terrace with an outside balcony to enjoy the views of the Andes. The 360° service leaves from Ollantaytambo station or Urubamba station and arrives at Aguas Calientes station. The travel time ranges from 1 hour

30 minutes to 2 hours, depending on the departure station. A one-way trip costs vary from $85 to $95 per person.

The First Class

The First Class service is the most premium and opulent option Inca Rail provides. It boasts exquisite carriages with leather seats, huge windows, baggage racks, air conditioning, heating, and aboard gourmet meals, superb wines, drinks, and live music included in the ticket price. The First Class service features a lounge car with a bar and an observation deck with an outside balcony. The First Class service leaves Ollantaytambo station and arrives at Aguas Calientes station. The trip time is 1 hour 45 minutes. The rates vary from $250 USD to $300 USD per person for a one-way trip.

Bimodal services (Bus plus Train)

Peru Rail and Inca Rail provide bimodal services combining bus and rail transportation to Machu Picchu. These services are available during the rainy season (from January to April) when the Poroy station is closed due to repair works or weather conditions. The bimodal services leave from

Wanchaq station (in Cusco) by bus and arrive at Ollantaytambo station by rail. From there, you can take any of the rail services described above to Aguas Calientes station. The trip duration ranges from 3 hours 30 minutes to 4 hours, depending on the train option you pick. The rates vary from $75 to $600 per person for a one-way ticket depending on the train service you pick.

Discount for a teen, the underage individual

Peru Rail and Inca Rail provide discounts for children under 12 who travel with an adult. The discount is 50% of the adult cost for all rail services except for the Hiram Bingham service, which does not accept children under 12 years old. To get the discount, you need to produce a valid passport or identification document of the kid at the time of booking and boarding.

Buying the tickets

You can purchase your train tickets online via the official websites of Peru Rail or Inca Rail or through approved travel agents or tour operators. You can purchase your train tickets at the railway stations or at the sales offices of Peru Rail or Inca Rail in Cusco or Lima. However, booking your train tickets in advance, particularly during peak season (from Can to September) or holidays (such as Easter or Christmas), is advisable since they tend to sell out rapidly owing to high demand.

Things to know before boarding your train

- You need to be at least 30 minutes before your departure time at the railway station to check in and board your train.

- You must submit your passport or identification document with your printed or electronic train ticket at the check-in desk.

- You can take one hand baggage of up to 5 kilograms (11 lb) and a maximum size of 157 cm (62 in).

- You are not permitted to take food or beverages on board save for water bottles.

- You are not permitted to smoke or use electrical devices that produce noises on board.

- You should wear comfortable clothing and shoes, sunscreen, sunglasses, a hat, and a raincoat, depending on the weather conditions.

- You are encouraged to drink lots of water before and throughout your travel to prevent altitude sickness.

- You are urged to appreciate the surroundings and relax throughout your travel.

Traveling to Machu Picchu by train is a terrific alternative for people who wish to appreciate the beauty and variety of the Andean scenery and the comfort and convenience of the train services. Traveling to Machu Picchu by train is an experience that will make your visit to this incredible wonder of the world even more unique.

Trek: choices, difficulty, and permits

One of the most gratifying and adventurous ways to visit Machu Picchu is via hiking through the breathtaking scenery of the Peruvian Andes. There are various routes, each with obstacles, attractions, and permits. Here is a suggestion prepared to help you organize your hiking journey to the old fortress.

The Inca Trail

The Inca Trail is the most renowned and popular journey to Machu Picchu. It follows a network of ancient roads that link several Inca monuments along the way, ending in the stunning entry via the Sun Gate. The typical Inca Trail is a 4-day/3-night journey that spans around 43 kilometers (26 mi) and reaches heights of up to 4,215 m (13,828 ft). You will travel through varied environments, from high mountains to cloud forests, and witness amazing ruins like Wiñay Wayna and Phuyupatamarca. It is a difficult hike that requires good fitness and acclimatization.

The Inca Trail needs a permit that must be obtained well in advance since there are only 500 permits available each day (including guides and porters). The Ministry of Culture grants the licenses, and can be acquired online or via an approved travel operator. The permits are non-transferable and non-refundable, and you must display your passport at the checkpoints along the path. The Inca Trail is closed in February for repairs.

The cost of the Inca Trail permit varies based on the season and the sort of service you pick. The usual price varies from $600 to $900 USD per person, which includes the admission fee to Machu Picchu, transportation, camping equipment, food, a guide, and porters. You can select services like extra porters, sleeping bags, or trekking poles.

The Salkantay Trek

The Salkantay Trek is an excellent alternative to the Inca Trail for those who prefer to escape the crowds and experience more diversified landscapes. The Salkantay Trek takes you around the beautiful Salkantay Mountain, one of the highest peaks in the Peruvian Andes at 6,271 m (20,574 ft). The journey is a 5-day/4-night walk that spans around 74 kilometers (46 mi) and reaches heights of up to 4,650 m (15,255 ft). You will cross varied landscapes, from glaciers and lakes to rainforests and coffee farms, and have the chance to visit hot springs and zip-line along the route. The Salkantay trip is considered tough, requiring a high degree of fitness and acclimatization.

The Salkantay Trek does not need a permit, but you must still plan your trip with a professional operator or guide. The cost of the Salkantay Trek varies based on the degree of comfort and service you pick. The usual price varies from $300 to $600 per person, which includes the admission ticket to Machu Picchu, transportation, camping equipment or lodgings, food, a guide, and horses. You can select services such as extra horses, sleeping bags, or trekking sticks.

The Lares Trek

The Lares Trek is another option to the Inca Trail that gives a more genuine cultural experience. The Lares Trek takes you through the secluded valleys and towns of the Lares area, where you can engage with the native Quechua people and learn about their traditions and customs. The Lares Trek is a 4-day/3-night trip that spans around 33 kilometers (20 mi) and reaches heights of up to 4,600 m (15,092 ft). You will experience breathtaking vistas of snow-capped mountains, waterfalls, lagoons, alpacas, and historic sites like Ollantaytambo and Pisac. The Lares trip is considered a moderate trip, requiring a decent degree of fitness and acclimatization.

The Lares Trek does not need a permit, but you still need to schedule your trip with a qualified operator or guide. The cost of the Lares Trek varies based on the degree of comfort and service you pick. The usual price varies from $400 to $700 USD per person, which includes the admission fee to Machu Picchu, transportation, camping equipment or hotels, food, a guide, and horses. You can select services such as extra horses, sleeping bags, or trekking sticks.

Other hiking possibilities

Numerous additional hiking choices to Machu Picchu appeal to varied interests, finances, and skills. Some of them are:

Choquequirao Trek: A 9-day/8-night trip exploring the's spectacular remains of Choquequirao, a sister city of Machu Picchu. This journey is exceedingly tough and isolated, demanding a high degree of fitness and acclimatization. No permission is necessary. However, the fee is significant owing to the length and difficulty of the walk.

Inca Jungle Trek: A 4-day/3-night trip that includes trekking, bicycling, rafting, and zip-lining to reach Machu Picchu. This journey is suited for thrill-seekers and novices since it does not include high heights or strenuous climbs. No permission is necessary. However, the cost is considerable owing to the diversity of activities and equipment involved.

Huchuy Qosqo Trek: A 3-day/2-night trip that explores the lesser-known remains of Huchuy Qosqo, a historic Inca palace overlooking the Sacred Valley. This walk is easy to moderate and gives an excellent introduction to the Inca culture and history. No permission is necessary, although the fee is cheap to moderate depending on the service and comfort level.

Summary

Trekking to Machu Picchu is a unique experience that enables you to immerse yourself in Peru's natural and cultural treasures. There are numerous alternatives, each with pros, drawbacks, and needs. The most crucial variables to consider while planning your expedition are:

- The availability and cost of licenses
- The difficulty and length of the journey
- The amount of fitness and acclimatization required
- The sort of service and comfort sought.
- The season and weather conditions

By researching and scheduling in advance, you can pick the ideal hike and experience a safe and exciting trip to Machu Picchu.

By car: benefits and drawbacks of driving to Machu Picchu

If you are seeking an exciting and picturesque method to travel to Machu Picchu, you can try driving there by automobile. This option allows you more freedom and independence and the ability to explore the breathtaking landscapes and cultures of the Sacred Valley and beyond. However, driving to Machu Picchu has problems and perils, so you must be well-equipped and educated before you hit the road.

How to drive to Machu Picchu

You can't drive to Machu Picchu since the citadel is only accessible by foot or bus from Aguas Calientes. The nearest you can reach by driving is the hydropower facility of Hidroelectrica, which is roughly 6 kilometers (3.7 miles) from Aguas Calientes. From there, you can walk along the railway lines or take a shuttle bus to the town.

To travel to Hidroelectrica by vehicle, you have two primary routes:

1. The first route is from Cusco, traveling via the villages of Urubamba and Ollantaytambo in the

Sacred Valley. This road is paved and well-maintained. However, it contains several twists and steep portions. It takes around 4 hours to reach Ollantaytambo, where you can tour some beautiful Inca sites and catch the train to Aguas Calientes. From Ollantaytambo, you continue on a gravel road to the Abra Malaga pass at 4,316 m (14,160 ft) above sea level, then descend through the rainforest area of Santa Maria and Santa Teresa. This route is narrow, uneven, and prone to landslides, particularly during the rainy season (November to March). It takes around 3 hours to reach Santa Teresa, where you can stay the night or continue for another hour to Hidroelectrica.

2. The second route is from Cusco, traveling via the villages of Chinchero and Urquillos in the Sacred Valley. This route is shorter but more strenuous since it traverses two high mountain passes: the Abra Amparaes at 4,461 m (14,636 ft) and the Abra Yanama at 4,668 m (15,315 ft). The route is largely unpaved and rugged, with hairpin curves and steep

dips. It takes roughly 6 hours to reach Hidroelectrica from Cusco on this route.

Pros of driving to Machu Picchu

- Driving to Machu Picchu offers various benefits over other types of transportation, such as:

- You can enjoy the spectacular beauty of the Andes and the Amazon jungle at your speed and stop anytime.

- You can explore additional sights along the journey, such as the Inca ruins of Ollantaytambo, Pisac, and Moray; the salt mines of Maras; the hot springs of Lares and Santa Teresa; and the coffee plantations of Quillabamba.

- You can save money on rail tickets, which can be pricey and sell out rapidly during high season.

- You can have greater flexibility and choice in selecting your route and lodging.

Cons of driving to Machu Picchu

1. Driving to Machu Picchu has several difficulties that you need to be aware of, such as:

2. You must have a valid driver's license and an international driving permit to drive in Peru. You need to have a trustworthy automobile with decent tires, brakes, and suspension, as well as a spare tire, a jack, a tool kit, and a first aid kit.

3. You must be an experienced driver who can manage high elevations, twisting roads, changeable weather conditions, and unexpected traffic. You need to be cautious of dangers such as potholes, rocks, animals, pedestrians, cyclists, and other cars.

4. You need to be prepared for situations such as flat tires, breakdowns, accidents, or road closures. Always bring adequate water, food, gasoline, cash, and a mobile phone. You should advise someone of your route and planned arrival time.

5. You need to observe the local norms and traditions while driving in Peru. You should always drive on the right side of the road, respect the speed limits and traffic signs, wear your seat belt, and avoid driving at night. You should be respectful to other drivers and pedestrians, particularly in rural regions where people can not be accustomed to automobiles.

Tips for driving to Machu Picchu

- If you opt to go to Machu Picchu by automobile, here is some advice that can help you have a safe and pleasurable trip:

- Book your vehicle hire in advance from a trustworthy business in Cusco. Check rates and reviews online or ask your hotel or travel agency for advice. You should verify the condition of the automobile and the insurance coverage before you sign the contract.

- Plan your route carefully, considering the distance, the driving time, the weather, and the road conditions. You should examine the availability and rates of motels, restaurants, and petrol stations along the road. You can utilize internet maps, guidebooks, or local advice to aid you with your planning.

- Pack light and smart, carrying just the basics for your vacation. You should also bring some warm clothing, a raincoat, a torch, a map, a compass, and a whistle in case of emergency. You should also allow some room in your vehicle for souvenirs and presents that you can purchase along the journey.

- Drive with caution and care, following the advice indicated above. You should also drive defensively, anticipating the activities of other drivers and avoiding confrontations or disagreements. You should also be courteous to the environment and the culture, avoiding littering, honking, or trespassing on private property.

- Enjoy the trip and the destination, soaking in the beauty and variety of Peru. You should also take advantage of the possibilities to mingle with the people and learn about their history, customs, and lifestyles. You should also realize the honor and responsibility of seeing one of the world's most stunning sights.

- Driving to Machu Picchu by vehicle is an alternative with some pros and downsides. It can be a wonderful and exciting way to discover Peru's different and magnificent landscapes and cultures, but it also demands a lot of preparation, expertise, and prudence. It is not a vacation for everyone, and you should carefully examine the advantages and downsides before deciding to take it.

CHAPTER 2

Exploring Machu Picchu

Machu Picchu is much more than simply a tourist destination. It is a holy location that unveils the secrets of a vanished civilization. It is a masterwork of engineering and construction that defies the laws of nature. It is a cultural gem that exhibits the variety and depth of the Andean world. It is a marvel that provokes astonishment, curiosity, and adoration.

Machu Picchu is one of the world's most recognizable and intriguing sites. It is a 15th-century Inca stronghold on a rocky slope in the Andes of Peru, overlooking the Urubamba River valley. It is a marvel of engineering and design, as well as a holy place that unveils the secrets and mysteries of the Inca civilization.

It was created by the Inca emperor Pachacuti as a royal estate and a religious center, but it was abandoned following the Spanish invasion. It remained concealed from the outer world until 1911 when it was unearthed by the American explorer Hiram Bingham.

This great tourist hub has several attractions and features that will astound you with their beauty and importance. You can visit its temples, palaces, terraces, fountains, and sculptures and learn about the Inca cosmology, astronomy, religion, and art. You can also trek to its neighboring peaks, Huayna Picchu and Machu Picchu Mountain, and enjoy panoramic views of the monument and the countryside. You can also explore its adjacent communities, like Aguas Calientes and Ollantaytambo, and sample the local culture and food.

In this chapter, we will lead you through experiencing Machu Picchu, from its major attractions to its hidden jewels, from its history to its tales, and from its practical recommendations to its best practices.

What to see and do at the Citadel of Machu Picchu

Machu Picchu is one of the world's most famous and awe-inspiring vistas. This old Inca city, hidden in the clouds and surrounded by beautiful mountains, is a tribute to the cunning and ability of the Inca culture. Whether you come by rail or by foot, you will be astounded by the grandeur and mystery of this UNESCO World Heritage Site.

How to get there

There are two major methods to travel to Machu Picchu: by train or climbing the Inca Trail. Both choices involve scheduling in advance and have varying pricing and perks.

By train

The most popular and easiest method to go to Machu Picchu is by taking a picturesque train trip from Cusco or Ollantaytambo. Various train services, such as PeruRail, IncaRail, and Belmond Hiram Bingham, provide varying degrees of comfort and cost. The train ride takes roughly 3.5 hours from Cusco and 1.5 hours from Ollantaytambo and goes through the magnificent Sacred Valley of the Incas.

The train will transport you to Aguas Calientes, commonly known as Machu Picchu Pueblo, which is the closest village to the citadel. From there, you must take a bus or climb for around 30 minutes to reach the entrance to Machu Picchu. The bus ticket costs $24 USD for a round journey and can be bought at the bus terminal in Aguas Calientes. The bus operates every 15 minutes from 5:30 am to 3:30 pm.

By trekking the Inca Trail

If you are daring and athletic, take the famed Inca Trail to Machu Picchu, one of the world's most stunning hikes. The Inca Trail is a 4-day journey with around 43 kilometers (26 miles) of ancient stone roads, mountain passes, and archaeological sites. You will need a permit to trek the Inca Trail, restricted to 500 per day and sell out rapidly. You must also join a certified tour operator supplying guides, porters, tents, food, and transportation.

The Inca Trail begins at Km 82 of the railway line at Ollantaytambo and finishes at the Sun Gate (Inti Punku), the entrance to Machu Picchu. Along the trip, you will enjoy beautiful vistas of the Andes Mountains, thick cloud forests, and spectacular Inca ruins. The walk's highlight is crossing the Dead Woman's Pass (Warmiwañusca), the highest point on the path at 4,200 m (13,779 ft) above sea level.

What to see

Machu Picchu is separated into two primary sectors: the urban and agricultural sectors. The urban sector encompasses most buildings and structures for religious, administrative, and residential functions. The agricultural area features terraces and granaries that were used for growing and storing food.

Some of the most noteworthy sights in Machu Picchu are:

- **The Temple of the Sun:** This circular edifice was devoted to Inti, the sun deity, and was utilized as an astronomical observatory. It features a huge window that corresponds with the winter solstice dawn.

- **The Intihuatana:** This carved stone pillar was used as a sundial and a holy location where the Incas chained the sun to keep it from going away.

- **The Temple of the Three Windows:** This rectangular temple has three trapezoidal windows that face east and give a panoramic view of the mountains. It depicts the three realms of life in Inca cosmology: Hanan Pacha (the above world), Kay Pacha (the terrestrial world), and Uku Pacha (the underworld).

- **The Temple of the Condor:** This tower includes two big rocks that mimic the wings of a condor, which was a holy animal for the Incas. It was utilized as a ceremonial altar and a jail.

- **The Main Plaza:** This huge open area was utilized for social events and ceremonies. It is bordered by the Principal Temple, the House of the High Priest, and the Royal Tomb.

- **The Royal Palace:** This complex of structures was the palace of Pachacuti, the Inca monarch who ordered the construction of Machu Picchu. It features a patio, a fountain, a bedroom, and a bathroom.

What to do

Besides seeing the citadel and learning about its history and culture, there are additional things that you can do at Machu Picchu:

- **Hike Huayna Picchu:** This steep peak rises behind the citadel and gives a bird's eye perspective of Machu Picchu. The walk takes around 2 hours round way and needs a special ticket that costs $15 and is restricted to 400 per day. You can select between two-time slots: 7:00 am to 8:00 am or 10:00 am to 11:00 am.

- **Hike Machu Picchu peak:** This peak overlooks the citadel and gives a panoramic view of the surrounding area. The walk takes around 3 hours round way and needs a special ticket that costs $15 and is restricted to 800 per day. You may select between two-time slots: 7:00 am to 8:00 am or 9:00 am to 10:00 am.

- Visit the Museum of Site Manuel Chávez Ballón: This museum is situated at the foot of Machu Picchu and shows relics, models, and images that illustrate the history and value of the site. The entry cost is $7, and the museum is open from 9:00 am to 4:30 pm.

- Relax at the hot springs of Aguas Calientes: After a hard day of touring Machu Picchu, you may rest in the natural thermal baths of Aguas Calientes. The hot springs are in the town center and feature multiple pools with varied temperatures. The admission cost is $6, and the hot springs are available from 5:00 am to 8:00 pm.

Where to stay

There are various alternatives for housing in Aguas Calientes, ranging from inexpensive hostels to luxury hotels. Here are some of the greatest places to stay near Machu Picchu:

- **Belmond Sanctuary Lodge:** This is the only hotel inside the Machu Picchu site, only steps away from the entrance. It provides big rooms with spectacular views, a restaurant, a bar, a spa, and a garden. The pricing each night begins at $1,000.

- **Inkaterra Machu Picchu Pueblo Hotel:** This lovely hotel replicates a typical Andean town with 12 acres of cloud forest. It features pleasant rooms with fireplaces, a restaurant, a bar, a spa, an orchid garden, and a tea house. The pricing each night begins at $500.

- **La Cabaña Machu Picchu:** This contemporary hotel is situated between the railway station and the bus stop. It provides nice rooms with balconies, a restaurant, a bar, a spa, and a patio. The pricing each night begins at $100.

- **Eco Quechua resort:** This eco-friendly resort is situated in the Mandor Valley, approximately 40 minutes away from Aguas Calientes by automobile. It provides rustic rooms with private toilets, a restaurant, a bar, a pool, and a garden. The pricing each night begins at $50.

When to go

- Machu Picchu is accessible all year round, but the ideal time to visit depends on your interests and money. The location has two primary seasons: the dry season (May to September) and the rainy season (October to April).

- Bright skies, mild temperatures, and low humidity characterize the dry season. It is also the peak season for tourists, which means higher costs and greater crowds. Frequent rains, foggy clouds, and colder temperatures mark the rainy season. It is also the low season for tourists, which means cheaper costs and fewer crowds.

- The optimal time to visit Machu Picchu is between the shoulder months of April and October when the weather is temperate and the crowds are modest.

How much does it cost?

The cost of visiting Machu Picchu varies based on your means of transportation, housing, activities, and personal spending. Here is an estimate of how much you may anticipate spending per person for a one-day visit:

- Train fare from Cusco or Ollantaytambo to Aguas Calientes: $60-$400 USD

- Bus fare from Aguas Calientes to Machu Picchu (round trip): $24 USD

- Entrance ticket to Machu Picchu (general admission): $70 USD

- Entrance ticket to Huayna Picchu or Machu Picchu Mountain (optional): $15 USD

- Food and beverages in Aguas Calientes: $20-$50

- Accommodation in Aguas Calientes (one night): $50-$1,000 USD

- Total cost (excluding tips and souvenirs): $229-$1,559

Tips for visiting Machu Picchu

Here are some essential ideas to make your journey to Machu Picchu more pleasurable and safe:

- Please book your tickets in advance online or via an approved agent since they tend to sell out fast. You can check the availability and costs of the tickets on the official website of Machu Picchu.

- Bring your passport and a printed ticket copy since you must present both at the door. You may also receive a Machu Picchu stamp on your passport as a keepsake.

- Hire a guide or join a group trip if you want to learn more about the history and culture of Machu Picchu. You may locate guides at the gate or book them online. The typical charge for a guide is $25 USD per person for a 2-hour trip.

- Respect the norms and regulations of Machu Picchu, such as not littering, not feeding the animals, not climbing on the walls, not using flash photography, and not bringing food, beverages, or bags bigger than 40 x 35 x 20 cm.

- Wear comfortable clothing and shoes, since you will be walking a lot and the weather might change suddenly. Bring a hat, sunglasses, sunscreen, bug repellent, and a raincoat or poncho.

- Stay hydrated and prevent altitude sickness by drinking lots of water and coca tea. Coca leaves are legal and commonly accessible in Peru, and they assist people in dealing with high elevation. You may also take medicine or oxygen if required.

- Enjoy the experience and snap plenty of photographs, but remember to put down your camera and admire the beauty and magic of Machu Picchu with your own eyes.

Conclusion

Machu Picchu is a place that will leave you speechless, astonished and fascinated. It is a marvel of engineering and design, a holy place of the Inca civilization, and a wonder of the globe. Visiting Machu Picchu is a once-in-a-lifetime event that you will never forget.

Whether you opt to ride the train or trek the Inca Trail, you will be rewarded with stunning vistas and intriguing insights into the culture and history of Machu Picchu. You will also get the chance to tour the fortress and uncover its secrets and mysteries.

There are numerous things to see and do at Machu Picchu, from viewing the Temple of the Sun and the Intihuatana to ascending Huayna Picchu and Machu Picchu Mountain to resting in the hot springs of Aguas Calientes. You will also discover a range of housing alternatives, from cheap hostels to luxury hotels, to meet your requirements and interests.

The ideal time to visit Machu Picchu is during the dry season or the shoulder months when the weather is lovely and the crowds are bearable. However, you may visit Machu Picchu any time of the year if you reserve your tickets in advance and obey the laws and restrictions.

How to join a tour

Machu Picchu is a place that ought to be visited and enjoyed with a guide or a tour. A guide or a tour may give you useful information, insights, and suggestions that will increase your experience and comprehension of the place and its history, culture, and importance. A guide or a tour can help you avoid the effort and worry of planning, arranging, and organizing your vacation and assure your safety and comfort. However, hiring a guide or joining a tour may also take time since numerous alternatives and aspects exist to consider. We have produced this guide with some valuable hints and recommendations to assist you in making the best selection.

Hiring a guide

If you want more freedom and independence in your visit, you may hire a guide who can accompany you and explain the site. A guide may be hired at the entrance to Machu Picchu or via your hotel or tour operator. A guide may also be booked online using Viator, GetYourGuide, or Klook services. A guided tour normally lasts approximately 2 hours and costs roughly 20 USD per person. However, the price and time may vary based on the guide's availability, expertise, and language abilities.

Some recommendations for hiring a guide are:

- **Check the guide's credentials:** A guide should have a valid license from the Ministry of Culture of Peru, confirming that they have finished a training course and passed an exam. A licensed guide should carry an official badge with their name and picture. You may also ask for their ID card or certificate to verify their identification and credentials.

- **Choose the language:** A guide should be able to speak your chosen language fluently and clearly. Most guides speak Spanish and English, but some also speak additional languages such as French, German, Italian, Portuguese, Japanese, or Chinese. Ask for a sample of their speech or read their reviews to check their language abilities.

- **Negotiate the price:** A guide may charge varying fees based on the season, demand, group size, and length of the trip. You may attempt to negotiate the price with the guide before hiring them, but be courteous and fair. If you are happy with their service, you may also tip the guide after the trip.

- **Please read the reviews:** A guide may have internet reviews from prior clients who have assessed their performance and comments. You may read these evaluations to understand the guide's personality, expertise, style, and dependability. You may also ask for suggestions from other visitors or locals who have hired guides previously.

Joining a tour

If you wish for more comfort and protection during your visit, you may join a tour that handles everything. A tour might include transportation, housing, admission tickets, food, guides, and activities. A tour may also provide numerous alternatives and packages based on your budget, tastes, and interests. A tour may be booked online using sites such as Expedia. Local agencies or operators in Cusco or Ollantaytambo may also organize a trip. A trip normally lasts from one to many days and costs 100 to 1000 USD per person. However, the price and length may vary based on the tour's schedule, quality, and exclusivity.

Some suggestions for joining a tour are:

- **Check the tour's reputation:** A tour should have a strong reputation and track record in the market. A respectable tour should have excellent evaluations from prior clients who have shared their experiences and thoughts. A credible tour should also include valid PromPeru, ASTA, or ATTA accreditations. You may also check whether the trip has any complaints or disputes filed against them.

- **Choose the type:** A trip should meet your requirements and expectations. There are numerous sorts of tours offered, such as:

1. **Classic tours:** These are trips that cover the key sites and features of Machu Picchu in a typical approach. They are appropriate for first-time visitors who wish to view the fundamentals of the site.

2. **Adventure tours:** These are trips that entail greater physical exercise and difficulty, such as hiking, bicycling, rafting, or zip-lining. They are excellent for daring guests who wish to experience more thrill and excitement.
3. **Cultural tours:** These excursions concentrate more on the history, culture, and customs of Machu Picchu and its surroundings. They are appropriate for interested tourists who wish to learn more about the location and its inhabitants.

4. **Luxury tours:** These trips provide extra luxury and exclusivity, such as private transportation, lodging in premium hotels or lodges, gourmet meals, VIP access to the destination, or exclusive activities. They are perfect for wealthier tourists who wish to experience greater luxury and convenience.

- **Compare the possibilities:** A tour may have numerous options and packages that vary in price, quality, and content. You should carefully analyze the alternatives and packages and select the best that matches your budget, tastes, and interests. You should also study the terms and conditions of the trip and verify what is included and what is not. You should also examine the cancellation and refund procedures of the trip in case of any modifications or exigencies.

How to escape the crowds and enjoy the scenery

Machu Picchu is a beautiful site that draws millions of people every year. However, this also means that it may become quite busy and loud, particularly during the peak season (June to August) during the peak hours (10 am to 2 pm). If you wish to escape the crowds and enjoy the vistas of Machu Picchu in peace and tranquillity, here are some tips and tactics that you may follow:

Book your tickets in advance: Machu Picchu has a restricted capacity of 2,500 visitors per day, and tickets sell out quickly. To reserve your seat, buy tickets online as soon as possible, ideally months in advance. You may purchase tickets through the official website or from approved travel companies. You should also print your tickets and carry them with you since the venue has no ticket office.

Choose the ideal time to visit: The greatest time to visit Machu Picchu depends on your tastes and priorities. If you want to escape the rain and enjoy the beautiful sky, you should come during the dry season (May to October). However, this is also the busiest and most costly period of the year. If you want to escape the crowds and save some money, you should come during the rainy season (November to April). However, this is also the riskiest period of the year since there may be landslides, road closures, and train disruptions. You should also check the weather prediction before you leave since things may change fast in the highlands.

Arrive early or stay late: The peak hours of Machu Picchu are between 10 am and 2 pm when most of the tour groups arrive and leave. If you want to beat the crowds and enjoy the dawn or sunset, you should come early or remain late. The facility opens at 6 am and closes at 5:30 pm. However, you may enter until 4 pm. You may board the first bus from Aguas Calientes at 5:30 am or the final bus at 3:30 pm. You may also trek up or down from Aguas Calientes, which takes approximately an hour and a half.

Explore beyond the major attractions: Machu Picchu offers numerous hidden jewels and secret sites that most tourists overlook or pass. If you wish to see more of the site and enjoy some tranquility, you should wander beyond the prominent attractions like the Temple of the Sun, the

Intihuatana Stone, and the prominent Plaza. You may visit the Inca Bridge, a tiny walkway that traverses a high cliff; the Temple of the Moon, a cave with carved niches; or the Sun Gate, a viewpoint that provides a panoramic view of Machu Picchu. You may also trek to Huayna Picchu or Machu Picchu Mountain, two peaks overlooking Machu Picchu. However, these walks need an additional ticket and a reservation since they have a restricted capacity of 400 guests daily.

Respect the laws and regulations: Machu Picchu is not merely a tourist attraction but a holy place and a cultural legacy. To maintain its beauty and integrity, you should observe the rules and restrictions of the site. You should not trash, smoke, consume alcohol, feed animals, touchstones, create noise, or snap selfies with sticks. You should also dress correctly, wear comfortable shoes, carry a small backpack, bring water and food, use sunscreen and bug protection, and stick on the defined trails.

By following these tips and methods, you may escape the crowds and enjoy the vistas of Machu Picchu in a more relaxing and polite manner. You may also have a more memorable and important experience that will last a lifetime.

CHAPTER 3

Staying near Machu Picchu

Machu Picchu, the ancient Inca fortress and one of the Seven Wonders of the World, is a must-see for every visitor visiting Peru. However, traveling to Machu Picchu is more complex than it sounds since it is situated high in the Andes Mountains, distant from any large city. Therefore, selecting where to stay near Machu Picchu is a vital choice that might affect your total experience.

You need to consider your money, time, interests, and travel plans when determining where to stay the night before or after viewing this incredible wonder of the world. There are two primary alternatives for accommodation near Machu Picchu: Aguas Calientes (Machu Picchu Pueblo) and Cusco.

Each choice has its perks and downsides, depending on what you are searching for. In this chapter, we will explore locations you may stay near Machu Picchu and help you make the best option for your trip.

Aguas Calientes: hotels, restaurants, and hot springs

Aguas Calientes, popularly known as Machu Picchu Pueblo, is the nearest village to the citadel of Machu Picchu. It is a tiny and vibrant town that provides various services and facilities for guests visiting the world-famous monument. You may find hotels, restaurants, stores, marketplaces, banks, and a railway station here. You may also enjoy the natural hot springs that give the town its name and unwind after a long day of touring.

Hotels

There are various alternatives for housing in Aguas Calientes, ranging from inexpensive hostels to luxury hotels. Here are some of the greatest places to stay near Machu Picchu:

- **Belmond Sanctuary Lodge:** This is the only hotel inside the Machu Picchu site, only steps away from the entrance. It provides big rooms with spectacular views, a restaurant, a bar, a spa, and a garden. The pricing each night begins at $1,000.

- **Inkaterra Machu Picchu Pueblo Hotel:** This lovely hotel replicates a typical Andean town with 12 acres of cloud forest. It features pleasant rooms with fireplaces, a restaurant, a bar, a spa, an orchid garden, and a tea house. The pricing each night begins at $500.

- **La Cabaña Machu Picchu:** This contemporary hotel is situated between the railway station and the bus stop. It provides nice rooms with balconies, a restaurant, a bar, a spa, and a patio. The pricing each night begins at $100.

- **Eco Quechua resort:** This eco-friendly resort is situated in the Mandor Valley, approximately 40 minutes away from Aguas Calientes by automobile. It provides rustic rooms with private toilets, a restaurant, a bar, a pool, and a garden. The pricing each night begins at $50.

Restaurants

A variety of cuisines and meals are served at many restaurants in Aguas Calientes. You may get regional specialties like lomo saltado (stir-fried beef with onions and tomatoes), ceviche (raw seafood marinated in lime juice), alpaca steak (lean and soft meat from the camelid), and quinoa (a healthy grain). You may also get foreign selections such as pizza, spaghetti, burgers, and sushi. Here are some of the greatest restaurants in Aguas Calientes:

- **Chullos Craft Beer & Home-Made Cuisine:** This nice and friendly restaurant provides Peruvian and nutritious cuisine with craft beer. You may enjoy fish ceviche, alpaca burger, quinoa salad, and chocolate cake. The average price per person is $15.

- **Mapacho Craft Beer Restaurant:** This sophisticated and energetic restaurant combines Peruvian and seafood cuisine with craft beer. You may taste meals such as octopus with huancaina sauce (a spicy cheese sauce), alpaca lomo saltado with elderberry sauce, and trout tiradito (thinly sliced fish with chili sauce). The average price per person is $20.

- **Fabrizzio's:** This bright and eccentric restaurant offers Peruvian and fusion meals with beverages. You may taste delicacies such as mushroom risotto, chicken curry, beef tenderloin with blue cheese sauce, and passion fruit cheesecake. The average price per person is $25.

- **KAYMANKA restaurant show:** This unique and exciting restaurant offers Peruvian and café cuisine with live music and dancing acts. You may sample delicacies such as chicken soup with noodles, stuffed peppers with cheese sauce, grilled fish with rice and salad, and fruit salad with yogurt. The average price per person is $10.

Hot springs

One of Aguas Calientes' primary attractions is the town center's natural hot springs. The volcanic activity of the area generates these pools and have varying temperatures ranging from 38°C to 46°C (100°F to 114°F). The water is a little yellow because of the sulfur, iron, and other minerals present. The hot springs are reputed to have medicinal characteristics and are great for calming your body and mind after seeing Machu Picchu.

The hot springs are open starting from 5:00 am to 8:00 pm every day. The admittance cost is $6 per person. There are changing facilities, showers, lockers, toilets, and snack bars accessible. You may also have massages and treatments for an added charge.

The hot springs are popular among residents and visitors alike, so they may sometimes become crowded and unclean. It is advisable to visit them early in the morning or late in the evening when they are less popular and cleaner. You should also bring your towel, swimwear, and flip-flops since they are neither supplied nor rented at the location.

Conclusion

Aguas Calientes is more than simply a gateway to Machu Picchu. It is a busy and picturesque town that provides a range of services and facilities for guests who wish to make the most of their stay. You can discover hotels, restaurants, stores, marketplaces, banks, and a railway station in Aguas

Calientes. You may also enjoy the natural hot springs in the town center and relax after a long day of exploration.

You will find it at Aguas Calientes, whether you are seeking a cheap hostel or a luxury hotel, a local specialty or international cuisine, a peaceful bath, or a massage. You will also discover nice and helpful individuals who will make you feel welcome and comfortable.

Camping: where to pitch your tent and what to bring

You can try camping if you are seeking a more adventurous and economical option to stay near Machu Picchu. Camping enables you to appreciate the natural beauty and tranquillity of the region, as well as the starry evenings and the early morning vistas. However, camping near Machu Picchu also has certain constraints and rules that you need to be aware of, so you need to be well-prepared and educated before you pitch your tent.

Where to camp near Machu Picchu

You can't camp within Machu Picchu since the citadel is only accessible from 6 am to 5:30 pm and has tight laws to maintain its conservation. The nearest you can camp is in Aguas Calientes, approximately 6 kilometers (3.7 miles) from Machu Picchu. There are a few camping possibilities in Aguas Calientes, such as:

- **Camping Machu Picchu:** This tiny and charming campsite is between the railway station and the bus stop. It provides tents for rent, or you may bring your own. It also offers restrooms, showers, power, Wi-Fi, lockers, and a kitchen. The fee is 15 soles (approximately $4) per person each night. It is open from 7 am until 10 pm. You may book online or by phone (+51 984 763 838).

- **Camping Ecologico:** This is a bigger and more spacious campground situated on the outskirts of the town, surrounded by nature and a river. It provides tents for rent, or you may bring your own. It also features restrooms, showers, power, Wi-Fi, a restaurant, a bar, and a pool. The fee is 20 soles (approximately $5) per person each night. It is open from 8 am until 11 pm. You may book online or by phone (+51 984 764 121).

- **Camping Los Jardines de Mandor:** This is a unique and serene campground near the Mandor Waterfalls, about 4 km (2.5 miles) from Aguas Calientes. It provides tents for rent, or you may bring your own. It also features restrooms, showers, power, Wi-Fi, a restaurant, a garden, and a walk to the waterfalls. The fee is 25 soles (approximately $6) per person each night. It is open from 8 am until 8 pm. You may book online or by phone (+51 984 791 213).

What to carry when camping near Machu Picchu

If you opt to camp near Machu Picchu, here are some items that you need to carry for your trip:

- **A tent:** You may hire one from the campsite or bring your own. If you bring your own, make sure it is lightweight, waterproof, and simple to put up and pack.

- **A sleeping bag:** You will need a warm and comfy sleeping bag since the evenings may be chilly and damp near Machu Picchu. You may either hire one from the campsite or bring your own.

- **A sleeping mat:** You will need a nice cushioned sleeping pad to protect you from the rough and uneven ground. You may either hire one from the campsite or bring your own.

- **A flashlight:** You will need a flashlight or a headlamp to see in the dark and navigate the campsite. You should also carry some backup batteries or a charger.

- **A backpack:** You will need a large, strong backpack to carry all your camping gear and personal things. You should also bring some plastic or ziplock bags to keep your items dry and orderly.

- **A water bottle:** You will need a reusable water bottle to remain hydrated throughout your vacation. You may refill it at the camp or the Machu Picchu water faucets.

- **A snack:** You will need food to keep your energy levels up throughout your journey. You may purchase some at the campsite or the stores in Aguas Calientes. Some nice possibilities include nuts, dried fruits, granola bars, chocolate, or cookies.

- **A camera:** You will need a camera to record your vacation's magnificent vistas and memories. You should also include some extra memory cards or a cloud storage service.

- **A passport:** You will need to access Machu Picchu and board the train or bus to return to Cusco. You should also duplicate it and store it in a secure location.

- **A ticket:** You will need your ticket to access Machu Picchu and enjoy any services or attractions there. You should also print it out or store it on your phone.

- **A handbook:** You will need a guidebook to understand more about the history, culture, and architecture of Machu Picchu. You may also hire a guide or join a tour if you like.

- **A hat:** You will need a hat to protect you from the sun and the rain throughout your vacation. You may also bring some sunglasses and sunscreen.

- **A jacket:** You will need a jacket to keep you warm and dry throughout your vacation. You may also bring some clothing and a raincoat.

- **A toiletries kit:** You will need a toiletry kit to keep yourself fresh. You should pack necessities such as a toothbrush, toothpaste, soap, shampoo, towel, deodorant, toilet paper, and wipes.

- **A first aid kit:** You will need one to cope with minor injuries or illnesses during your vacation. You should pack some necessities such as bandages, antiseptic, painkillers, anti-inflammatory, anti-diarrhea, anti-nausea, and altitude sickness medicines.

Tips for camping near Machu Picchu

If you opt to camp near Machu Picchu, here are some guidelines that can help you have a safe and fun trip:

- Book your campsite in advance since they may fill up rapidly during the high season. You may also check the reviews and ratings of the campsites online or ask your hotel or travel agency for advice.

- Plan your route carefully, considering the distance, the time, the weather, and the availability of the services and attractions. You should also examine the opening and closing hours of Machu Picchu and the campsites.

- Pack light and smart, carrying just the basics for your vacation. You should also bring warm clothing, a raincoat, a torch, a map, a compass, and a whistle in an emergency. You should also allow some room in your bag for souvenirs and presents that you may purchase along the journey.

- Camp safely and carefully, observing the norms and regulations of the campsites and Machu Picchu. You should also respect the environment and the culture, avoiding littering, causing noise, or trespassing on private property.

- Enjoy the experience and the adventure, soaking in the beauty and quiet of the surroundings. You should also take advantage of the possibilities to mingle with the people and learn about their history, customs, and lifestyles. You should also realize the honor and responsibility of seeing one of the world's most stunning sights.

Camping near Machu Picchu is an option that provides some pros and downsides. It may be a wonderful and economical way to appreciate the natural beauty and quiet of the region, but it also demands a lot of planning and research. It is only a choice for some, and you should carefully examine the advantages and drawbacks before you pitch your tent.

Luxury options

If you are searching for a nice and pleasant hotel near Machu Picchu, you have two alternatives: Belmond Sanctuary Lodge and Inkaterra Machu Picchu Pueblo Hotel. Both hotels provide world-class service, delicious food, and beautiful views of the Andean environment. Here are some information about each hotel:

- **Belmond Sanctuary Lodge:** This hotel is close to Machu Picchu. You may have direct access to the historic citadel before sunrise and beat the crowds. You may also appreciate the magnificent mountains and forest views from your accommodation or the patio. The hotel includes 31 rooms and suites equipped with cable TV, iPod docking stations, air conditioning, and private bathrooms. The hotel also has a bar, a spa, a garden, and two dining options. The motel is open 24 hours a day, seven days a week. The costs vary from $1,500 to $2,500 per night, depending on the hotel's season and style. The hotel has a rating ranging from 4.5 out of 5 stars.

- **Inkaterra Machu Picchu Pueblo Hotel:** This hotel is situated in Aguas Calientes, the village at the foot of Machu Picchu. It is a 10-minute bus ride or a 1.5-hour walk from the citadel. The hotel is constructed like a typical Andean town, with 83 casitas (cottages) situated within 12 acres of cloud forest. The casitas offer fireplaces, patios, and private bathrooms. Some of them even feature plunge pools or jacuzzis. The hotel also contains a restaurant, a café, a bar, a spa, an orchid garden, and a tea plantation. The hotel is open from 6:00 am to 10:00 pm every day. The costs vary from $600 to $1,200 each night, depending on the season and the style of the casita. The hotel's rating is 4.5 star.

Both hotels are wonderful alternatives for guests who wish to see Machu Picchu in luxury and comfort. They provide varied facilities and atmospheres, so you may select the one that meets your interests and budget.

CHAPTER 4

Beyond Machu Picchu

Beyond Machu Picchu is a location that provides much more of Machu Picchu. It is a destination where you may immerse yourself in the rich history, culture, and environment of the Andean continent. It is a site where you can experience the richness and beauty of Peru, from its ancient ruins and customs to its contemporary attractions and inventions. It is a location where you may discover adventure, leisure, or study, depending on your choices and requirements.

Machu Picchu is one of many sights in the Sacred Valley of the Incas. There are many additional attractions and activities that you may enjoy in this area, which is rich in history, culture, and environment. You can explore other amazing Inca fortifications, such as Huayna Picchu and Machu Picchu Mountain, and learn about their history and importance. You may enjoy various interesting and adventurous activities, such as rafting, bicycling, hiking, horseback riding, yoga, meditation, culinary courses, and cultural excursions.

In this chapter, we will guide you through some of the greatest alternatives that you may select from to make your vacation more fun and memorable.

Huayna Picchu: how to climb the legendary peak

Suppose you seek an additional challenge and a fresh view of Machu Picchu, the ancient Inca fortress and one of the Seven Wonders of the World. In that case, you should explore climbing Huayna Picchu, the famous mountain that rises above the site. Huayna Picchu, a youthful mountain in Quechua, is a steep and rocky peak with amazing views of Machu Picchu and the surrounding valleys. However, climbing Huayna Picchu is difficult for the faint-hearted since it needs a decent degree of fitness, agility, and guts. Here is all you need to know about how to climb Huayna Picchu.

Address

Huayna Picchu is situated inside the Machu Picchu archaeological complex in the Cusco region of Peru. The entrance to Huayna Picchu lies near the Sacred Rock, at the northern end of Machu Picchu.

Opening time and closing time

Huayna Picchu is available every day from 7:00 am to 2:00 pm. However, two groups of 200 hikers each are permitted to climb Huayna Picchu daily. The first group begins at 7:00 am, and the second group starts at 10:00 am. You have to pick your group when you purchase your ticket. You must arrive at the entry gate at least 15 minutes before your designated time. You also have to sign in and exit at the entry gate.

Prices with ratings

The fee to climb Huayna Picchu is $75 per person for visitors and $37 per person for Peruvians and foreign citizens. This price includes the admission charge to Machu Picchu and Huayna Picchu. You have to purchase your ticket in advance since there are only 400 seats available every day, and they tend to sell out fast. You may purchase your ticket online via the official website of the Ministry of Culture [https://www.actionperutreks.com/machu-picchu-trips/all-about-that-other-permit-a-k-a-huayna-picchu/]1 or through approved travel agencies or tour operators [https://flipflopsincluded.com/huayna-picchu-hike/].

Most hikers feel that ascending Huayna Picchu is a pleasant and thrilling experience that gives great vistas and a sense of achievement. However, several hikers also caution that ascending Huayna Picchu is complex and might be deadly if you are prepared and vigilant. Some of the problems and hazards include:

- **The height:** Huayna Picchu reaches an elevation of 2,720 meters (8,920 feet) above sea level, which might induce altitude sickness if you need to be sufficiently acclimatized.

- **The steepness:** Huayna Picchu has an elevation rise of roughly 300 meters (984 feet) from the base to the top, which means you have to climb steep stone steps for much of the way.

- **The narrowness:** Huayna Picchu has certain areas where the steps are narrow and have no handrails or protection. You have to be cautious not to slide or fall.

- **The exposure:** Huayna Picchu has certain places where you are exposed to cliffs and fall on both sides. You have to be courageous and not look down if you suffer from vertigo or fear heights.

- **The weather:** Huayna Picchu may be impacted by rain, fog, wind, or heat, depending on the season and time of day. You have to be prepared for any weather situation and dress properly.

Therefore, to climb Huayna Picchu, you must be in excellent physical form, have a positive attitude, obey the safety guidelines, and enjoy the journey.

Machu Picchu Mountain: an alternate walk with spectacular vistas

If you seek a tough and rewarding climb that gives spectacular views of Machu Picchu and the surrounding mountains, you should attempt Machu Picchu Mountain. This trek is less busy and more picturesque than the famed Huayna Picchu, and it brings you to the highest point in the vicinity, where you can enjoy a 360-degree panoramic of the old Inca fortress and the holy valley.

Machu Picchu Mountain, also known as Montaña or Old Mountain, is situated on the other side of Huayna Picchu, southwest of the main ruins. It is a steep and arduous journey that entails ascending more than 2,000 stone stairs and reaching over 600 meters in height. The trek takes around 3 hours, with some time to see the views at the peak.

To trek Machu Picchu Mountain, you must acquire a unique combo ticket that covers both admission to Machu Picchu and access to the mountain. You may acquire this ticket online or via an approved agency in advance since there is a restricted capacity of 800 persons daily. The ticket costs 200 soles (about 50 USD) for foreigners and 64 soles (about

16 USD) for Peruvians. You also need to pick between two slots: from 7 am to 8 am or 9 am to 10 am. You can only access the mountain between these periods. However, you may remain as long as you like till 3 pm.

The trailhead for Machu Picchu Mountain is situated around 15 minutes walk from the main gate to Machu Picchu via the sanctuary. You need to follow the signs for Intipunku (Sun Gate) and then turn right at a fork. You will approach a checkpoint where you must present your passport and ticket. From there, you will start your trek on a well-marked but narrow trail that zigzags up the mountain.

The trek is tough yet rewarding, as you will travel through numerous ecosystems and sceneries, such as cloud forests, grassland, and rocky terrain. You will also view various Inca ruins and terraces along the journey and some animals like hummingbirds, butterflies, and flowers. Trees generally cover the trek, but it may become hot and humid, so carry extra water, sunscreen, hat, and bug repellent.

The highlight of the trek is reaching the peak of Machu Picchu Mountain, where you will be rewarded with a beautiful panorama of Machu Picchu and the surrounding mountains. You can view the full site from above, the Urubamba River, and the Sacred Valley below. You will also experience a feeling of success and amazement for being at one of the highest places in the region. You may spend some time at the peak to snap photographs, relax, meditate, or enjoy the panorama.

The trek back down is easier but needs attention since the stairs may be slick and steep. You must be cautious not to twist your ankle or knee and give way to other hikers heading up. You will approach the checkpoint again, where you must sign out with your passport and ticket. From there, you may return to Machu Picchu or visit other regions of the site.

Machu Picchu Mountain is an alternate walk that gives a distinct view and experience of Machu Picchu. It is a tough but rewarding trek that needs strong physical conditioning and preparedness. It is also a less busy and more picturesque trek than Huayna Picchu, and it leads you to the highest point in the region, where you can enjoy a panoramic view of Machu Picchu and the surrounding mountains. If you seek an adventure and a challenge that will make your vacation to Machu Picchu unique, you may want to explore trekking Machu Picchu Mountain.

Address: Machu Picchu Mountain Trailhead Opening time: 7 am Closing time: 3 pm Prices: 200 soles (about 50 USD) for foreigners; 64 soles (about 16 USD) for Peruvians Ratings: ☐☐☐☐☐

To summarize, Machu Picchu Mountain is an alternate walk that gives a new view and experience of Machu Picchu. It is a tough but rewarding trek that needs strong physical conditioning and preparedness. It is also a less busy and more picturesque trek than Huayna Picchu, and it leads you to the highest point in the region, where you can enjoy a panoramic view of Machu Picchu and the surrounding mountains. If you seek an adventure and a challenge that will make your vacation to Machu Picchu unique, you may want to explore trekking Machu Picchu Mountain.

The Sun Gate and the Inca Bridge: simple treks with historical importance

Machu Picchu is not simply a wonder of building and engineering but also a site of spiritual and cultural importance. The Incas erected this castle as a holy sanctuary for their sun deity, Inti, and a shelter for their elite. To reach and safeguard this secret metropolis, they erected many roads and buildings that are still visible today. The Sun Gate (Inti Punku) and the Inca Bridge (Qhapaq Chaka) are two of the most noteworthy ones.

The Sun Gate

The Sun Gate is a stone archway that marks the entrance to Machu Picchu from the Inca Trail. It is situated on the southeast side of the site, at a height of 2,720 m (8,924 ft). It gives a wonderful view of the castle and the surrounding mountains.

The Sun Gate got its name from its alignment with the sun on the winter solstice, when the sun rises directly above the gate. It was also utilized as an astronomical observatory and a ceremonial altar by the Incas. The Sun Gate was guarded by soldiers who controlled the approach to Machu Picchu.

The Sun Gate may be accessed by trekking from Machu Picchu or joining one of the Inca Trail trips. The trek from Machu Picchu takes around 2 hours and is quite tough. The path is largely uphill and includes some steep spots. The trek from the Inca Trail takes around 4 hours and is easy to moderate. The pathway is primarily downhill and follows the old stone road of the Incas.

The Sun Gate is open from 6:00 am to 5:00 pm every day. There is no extra payment to see the Sun Gate, but you must have a valid ticket to Machu Picchu or the Inca Trail. You must also carry your passport and a printed copy of your ticket.

The Inca Bridge

The Inca Bridge is a wooden plank bridge that traverses a tiny gap on the west side of Machu Picchu. It is situated at a height of 2,650 m (8,694 ft). It gives a breathtaking perspective of the high cliff and the Urubamba River below.

The Inca Bridge was part of a secret path that linked Machu Picchu with other nearby Inca structures. It was utilized as an escape route in case of an assault or an invasion. The bridge was meant to be quickly disassembled by taking out certain wooden planks, leaving behind a gap that was hard to traverse.

The Inca Bridge may be accessed by trekking from Machu Picchu. The trek takes around 1 hour round way and is simple to moderate. The path is largely level and includes occasional stairs and tight parts. The climb is not recommended for anyone who have vertigo or a fear of heights.

The Inca Bridge is available from 7:00 am to 4:00 pm every day. There is no extra payment to see the Inca Bridge, but you must have a valid ticket to Machu Picchu. You must also sign a register at the gate and respect other safety restrictions, such as not crossing the bridge or taking pictures.

Conclusion

The Sun Gate and the Inca Bridge are two of the most amazing features of Machu Picchu. They demonstrate the brilliance and skill of the Incas, as well as their relationship with nature and their gods. They also provide breathtaking vistas and fascinating experiences for tourists who wish to explore more of this ancient treasure.

If you seek simple treks with historical value, you should take advantage of these two sights when visiting Machu Picchu. You will be surprised by their beauty and mystery, and you will discover more about the culture and history of the Incas.

CHAPTER 5

Cusco and the Sacred Valley

Cusco and the Sacred Valley are two of Peru's most intriguing and unique places. They are the heart and spirit of the Andean culture, where you may discover the past of the Inca Empire, the colonial heritage, and the present existence. They are also the entryway to Machu Picchu, the country's most renowned and visited destination.

Cusco is a city that mixes history, art, and architecture mesmerizingly. It was the capital of the Inca Empire, and it still maintains many of its structures, temples, and palaces. It was also the Spanish conquest's capital, with several spectacular cathedrals, churches, and houses. It is a dynamic and cosmopolitan city with various museums, marketplaces, restaurants, pubs, and festivals.

The Sacred Valley is a territory that runs along the Urubamba River from Pisac to Ollantaytambo. It is a rich and picturesque valley with verdant farmland, snow-capped mountains, and colorful settlements. It is home to various archaeological monuments, like Pisac, Ollantaytambo,

Moray, and Maras, that highlight the brilliance and complexity of the Inca civilization. It is also a popular destination for outdoor activities such as hiking, bicycling, rafting, horseback riding, and yoga.

In this chapter, we will lead you through Cusco and the Sacred Valley, providing full information on how to get there, what to see and do, where to stay and eat, and what to anticipate. We will also provide some ideas and tactics for making your vacation more fun and memorable. Whether searching for culture, nature, or adventure, you will find it in Cusco and the Sacred Valley.

Cusco: the historic capital of the Inca Empire and a UNESCO World Heritage Site

Cusco, often called Cuzco or Qosqo, is South America's oldest continuously inhabited city and the entrance to Machu Picchu. It was formerly the Inca Empire's majestic capital, spanned from Colombia to Chile. It is today a bustling and cosmopolitan metropolis that mixes old and colonial past with contemporary and indigenous culture. It is also a UNESCO World Heritage Site since 1983, recognized for its historical, architectural, and cultural importance.

Cusco is a must-see location for anybody visiting Peru, as it provides a plethora of sights, activities, and experiences that will capture and fascinate you. Here are some of the highlights that you should not miss:

How to get to Cusco

The simplest and quickest method to arrive at Cusco is via flying. The Alejandro Velasco Astete International Airport is approximately 5 kilometers (3 miles) from the city center and gets daily flights from Lima, Arequipa, Puno, Puerto Maldonado, and other domestic locations. There are also a few international flights from La Paz (Bolivia), Bogota (Colombia), and Santiago (Chile). You may book your flights online or via a travel agency.

You may take a cab, bus, or shuttle to your hotel or hostel from the airport. The cab price is roughly 10-15 soles (about $3-4) and takes about 15 minutes. The bus price is roughly 1 sol (about $0.25) and takes 30 minutes. The shuttle ticket is roughly 5 soles (about $1.5) and takes about 20 minutes. You may locate them outside the airport terminal.

Another method to go to Cusco is via bus. Various bus companies run from Lima, Arequipa, Puno, Nazca, and other locations in Peru. Bus travel may take 10 to 24 hours, depending on the route and the traffic. The bus ticket varies from 50 to 200 soles (approximately $14-57) depending on the service and the comfort level. You may book your tickets online or at the bus station.

The major bus port in Cusco is named Port Terrestre and is situated around 3 kilometers (1.8 miles) from the city center. You may take a cab, bus, or shuttle to your hotel or hostel from there. The cab price is roughly 5-10 soles (about

$1.5-3) and takes 10 minutes. The bus price is roughly 1 sol (about $0.25) and takes about 20 minutes. The shuttle ticket is roughly 5 soles (about $1.5) and takes 15 minutes. You may locate them outside the terminal building.

What to see and do in Cusco

There are many things to see and do in Cusco, whether you are interested in history, culture, art, or adventure. Here are some of the most popular sights and activities in Cusco:

The Plaza de Armas: This is the main plaza of Cusco, where you can observe the majestic Cathedral, the Church of La Compañía de Jesús, and the colonial arcades surrounding it. It is also the heart of social and cultural life, where you can find restaurants, cafés, bars, boutiques, and street performers. It is most busy at night when it is lit with multicolored lights.

The Qoricancha: This is the holiest temple of the Incas, devoted to the sun deity Inti. It was previously coated with gold and silver, but the Spanish invaders took much of it. They then erected the Church of Santo Domingo on top of it, providing a stunning contrast between Inca and Catholic architecture. You may visit the temple and the church with a single ticket, which costs 15 soles (about $4) for foreigners and 5 soles (about $1) for Peruvians. The opening hours are Monday to Saturday from 8:30 am to 5:30 pm and Sunday from 2 pm to 5 pm.

The Sacsayhuaman: This is a large stronghold that overlooks Cusco from a height. It was created by the Incas using large stones that fit together precisely without any mortar. It was also the location of a devastating fight between the Incas and the Spanish in 1536. You may explore its walls, towers, tunnels, and slides and enjoy panoramic views of the city. You need to obtain the Cusco Tourist Ticket to visit this site, which costs 130 soles (about $35) for foreigners and 70 soles (about $19) for Peruvians. It permits you to explore 16 more sights in Cusco and adjacent valleys within ten days. The opening hours are Monday to Sunday from 7 am to 5:30 pm.

The San Blas is a lovely bohemian area on a high slope behind the Plaza de Armas. It is noted for its tiny cobblestone alleys, colorful buildings, creative workshops, and quiet cafés. It is also home to the San Blas Church, which boasts a stunning carved wooden pulpit that is regarded as one of Peru's greatest specimens of colonial art. You may enter the church with a contribution of 15 soles (approximately $4), which includes an audio tour. The opening hours starts from 9 am to 5 pm, Monday to Saturday.

The San Pedro Market: This vibrant and colorful market sells everything from fresh fruits and veggies to souvenirs and handicrafts. It is also a fantastic spot to enjoy some local specialties such as cuy (guinea pig), chiriuchu (a cold dish with different meats), or chicha morada (a purple corn drink). You may also discover several affordable and good eateries within the market that offer characteristic foods like ceviche, lomo saltado, or aji de gallina. The market is open every day starting from 6 am until 6 pm.

These are just a few of the numerous things that Cusco has to offer. You may also visit other museums, cathedrals, and ancient sites or take day excursions to adjacent towns like Maras, Moray, Pisac, or Ollantaytambo. You will always have things to do and see in this beautiful city.

Where to stay and dine in Cusco

Cusco provides a broad choice of lodging alternatives for every budget and inclination. You may find hotels, hostels, guesthouses, flats, or campsites in various city sections. Here are some of the greatest places to stay in Cusco:

Palacio del Inka: This luxury hotel occupies an ancient Inca palace and monastery. It provides magnificent rooms with colonial design, contemporary conveniences, and views of the city or the courtyard. It also features a spa, a restaurant, a bar, and a museum. The price is roughly $200 per night for a double room.

Tierra Viva Cusco Plaza is a mid-range hotel near the Plaza de Armas. It provides pleasant rooms with hardwood flooring, colorful carpets, and private bathrooms. It also features a breakfast area, a balcony, and a laundry service. The price is roughly $60 per night for a double room.

Kokopelli Hostel Cusco: This is a cheap hostel in the San Blas area. It provides dormitories and private rooms with shared or ensuite bathrooms. It also features a kitchen, a bar, a lounge, and a garden. The price is roughly $10 per night for a bed in a dorm or $30 per night for a separate room.

Cusco also provides a vast choice of eating alternatives for taste and hunger. You may discover restaurants, cafés, pubs, street stalls, or marketplaces that offer local, national, or international food. Here are some of the greatest places to eat in Cusco:

- **Chicha:** This is a gourmet restaurant led by the renowned chef Gaston Acurio. It delivers unique cuisine based on traditional Peruvian ingredients and tastes. Some of the delicacies include alpaca carpaccio, quinoa risotto, or guinea pig confit. The fee is roughly $25 per person.

- **Pachapapa:** This is a rustic restaurant in the San Blas district. It provides genuine cuisine prepared in wood-fired ovens or clay pots. Some of the delicacies include pachamanca (meat and vegetables cooked underground with hot stones), cuy al horno (roasted guinea pig), or trucha al horno (baked fish). The fee is $15 per person.

- **Jack's café:** This quaint café is popular with residents and visitors alike. It provides substantial breakfasts, sandwiches, salads, burgers, soups, and desserts. Some favorites include banana pancakes, chicken avocado sandwiches, quinoa salad, or chocolate cake. The fee is roughly $10 per person.

Cusco is not just a historical and cultural gem but also a dynamic and enjoyable place that will make you fall in love with its people, cuisine, music, and energy. It is a city that will amaze you with its variety and charm and make you feel at home.

Ollantaytambo: a picturesque village with spectacular ruins and a railroad station

Ollantaytambo, or Ollanta for short, is a small and scenic village in the Sacred Valley of Peru, roughly midway between Cusco and Machu Picchu. It is not just a handy stopover for visitors traveling to the Inca citadel but also a location worth experiencing in its own right.

Ollantaytambo has some of the most stunning and best-preserved Inca ruins in Peru and is a lovely ancient city that preserves its original Inca layout and architecture. Ollantaytambo is also a cultural hotspot that shows the rich and varied traditions of the local people, who still speak Quechua and wear colorful clothing.

Ollantaytambo has a rich and intriguing history that extends back to the Inca Empire when it was a significant administrative and religious center. It was also the scene of one of the rare Inca successes over the Spanish invaders, headed by the insurgent commander Manco Inca in 1537. Today, Ollantaytambo is a living museum that unveils the mysteries of the past and the energy of the present.

How to go to Ollantaytambo

There are numerous methods to go to Ollantaytambo from Cusco or Machu Picchu, depending on your money, time, and inclination. Here are some of the most prevalent options:

By train: This is the simplest and most pleasant method to travel to Ollantaytambo, particularly if you are coming from or heading to Machu Picchu. Two railway companies operate from Ollantaytambo: PeruRail1 and Inca Rail. They provide diverse services and pricing, ranging from $25 to $100 per person one way. You may book your tickets online or at the railway station. The train travel takes roughly 1.5 hours from Cusco or 2 hours from Machu Picchu.

By bus: This is the cheapest and most flexible method to travel to Ollantaytambo, particularly if you are coming from or heading to Cusco. Various bus companies run from Cusco's major bus terminal (Terminal Terrestre) or smaller stations around the Plaza de Armas. For one trip, they charge roughly 10 soles (about $3) per person. You may purchase your tickets on the spot or in advance. The bus travel takes roughly 2 hours from Cusco.

By taxi: This is the quickest and most convenient way to get to Ollantaytambo, particularly if you travel with baggage or in a group. You can locate cabs at the airport, the railway station, or the bus terminal in Cusco or Machu Picchu. They charge roughly 80-100 soles (about $22-28) for each vehicle for one trip. You may discuss the journey's price and length with the driver. The cab travel takes roughly 1 hour from Cusco or 1.5 hours from Machu Picchu.

By tour: This is the ideal way to travel to Ollantaytambo if you want to see more of the Sacred Valley. Various travel organizations provide day excursions or multi-day packages that include Ollantaytambo and other destinations like Pisac, Moray, Maras, Chinchero, or Urubamba. They charge roughly $50-100 per person, depending on the route and the service. You may book your tour online or via your hotel or travel agency.

What to see and do in Ollantaytambo

There are many things to see and do in Ollantaytambo, whether you are interested in history, culture, nature, or adventure. Here are some of the highlights that you should not miss:

The Ollantaytambo Ruins: These are the major attraction of Ollantaytambo and are one of Peru's most magnificent and well-preserved Inca monuments. They comprise a castle, a temple, terraces, storehouses, fountains, and baths erected by the Inca monarch Pachacuti in the 15th century. Manco Inca also utilized them as a fortification during his rebellion against the Spanish in 1537. You may tour the remains independently or with a guide, who will explain their history, architecture, and meaning. You need to obtain the Cusco Tourist Ticket to visit this site, which costs 130 soles (about $35) for foreigners and 70 soles (about $19) for Peruvians. It permits you to explore 16 more sights in Cusco and adjacent valleys within ten days. The opening hours are Monday to Sunday from 7 am to 5:30 pm.

The Ollantaytambo Town: This is the historic core of Ollantaytambo and one of the few sites in Peru that still has its original Inca layout and architecture. You may wander through the tiny cobblestone alleys, see the stone walls and canals, visit the colonial churches and museums, and buy at the local markets and artisan booths. You may also connect with the welcoming inhabitants, who still wear traditional clothing and speak Quechua. The town is free to visit and open all day.

The Pinkuylluna Mountain: This hill rises above the Ollantaytambo town and gives spectacular views of the valley and the ruins. It is also home to several Inca storehouses used to store food and harvests at high altitudes. You may trek up to the mountain's summit on a well-marked track, which takes approximately an hour. The trek is free and accessible all day, but you should bring comfortable shoes, sunscreen, and a hat.

The Ollantaytambo Train Station is the primary train station in Ollantaytambo and one of the most convenient routes to reach Machu Picchu. It is approximately 1 km (0.6 miles) from the town center and features a ticket office, a waiting area, baggage storage, a café, and a souvenir store. From here, take the train to Aguas Calientes, the settlement at the foot of Machu Picchu. The train travel takes around 2 hours and costs between $25-100 per person one way, depending on the service and the season. You may book your tickets online or at the station.

Where to stay and eat in Ollantaytambo

Ollantaytambo boasts a broad choice of hotel alternatives for any budget and inclination. You may find hotels, hostels, guesthouses, flats, or campsites in various locations in the town. Here are some of the greatest places to stay in Ollantaytambo:

El Albergue: This beautiful hotel is situated within the railway station, making it extremely handy for guests traveling to Machu Picchu. It provides small rooms with hardwood flooring, private bathrooms, and views of the garden or the mountains. It also features a restaurant, a bar, a spa, a farm, and a coffee roastery. The price is roughly $100 per night for a double room.

Mama Simona: This is a modest hostel in the town center, making it quite accessible for guests exploring Ollantaytambo. It provides dormitories and private rooms with shared or ensuite bathrooms. It also features a kitchen, a lounge, a garden, and a laundry service. The price is roughly $10 per night for a bed in a dorm or $30 per night for a separate room.

Sol Natura: This is a unique guesthouse situated on the town's outskirts, making it quite serene and pleasant for tourists searching for some serenity. It provides big rooms with private bathrooms, patios, and hammocks. It also features a restaurant, a pool, a yoga studio, and a massage service. The price is roughly $50 per night for a double room.

Ollantaytambo also boasts many culinary alternatives for any taste and hunger. You may discover restaurants, cafés, pubs, street stalls, or marketplaces that offer local, national, or international food. Here are some of the greatest places to eat in Ollantaytambo:

Apu Veronica: This gourmet restaurant delivers unique recipes based on fresh foods from their garden. Some delicacies include fish ceviche, alpaca steak, or quinoa pudding. The fee is roughly $20 per person.

Hearts café: This is a pleasant café that provides substantial breakfasts, sandwiches, salads, soups, and desserts. Some favorites include banana pancakes, chicken avocado sandwiches, quinoa salad, or carrot cake. The fee is roughly $10 per person.

Puka Rumi: This rustic restaurant provides genuine cuisine cooked in clay pots over a wood fire. Some of the delicacies include pachamanca (meat and vegetables cooked underground with hot stones), cuy al horno (roasted guinea pig), or trucha al horno (baked fish). The fee is $15 per person.

Ollantaytambo is not just a picturesque town with stunning ruins and a railway station but also a cultural center that shows the rich and diversified customs of the local people who still speak Quechua and wear colorful clothing.

Pisac: a vibrant market and a high fortification

Pisac is a picturesque village in the Sacred Valley of Peru, approximately 33 kilometers (20 miles) northeast of Cusco. It is notable for its colorful market and its hilltop stronghold, both of which highlight the rich history and culture of the Inca civilization. Pisac is a terrific spot to visit for those who wish to see the real and traditional side of Peru and appreciate the Andes' beautiful grandeur.

Here are some information about Pisac:

How to get there: Pisac can be accessed by bus, taxi, or tour from Cusco. The bus takes around an hour and costs 4 soles (about $1) for each passenger. The bus terminal is at Puputi Street in Cusco, and the buses depart every 15 minutes from 6 am to 6 pm. The cab takes around 45 minutes and costs roughly 80 soles (about $20) for every journey.

You may get cabs to Plaza de Armas or Plaza San Francisco in Cusco or reserve one online. The trip takes around half a day and costs roughly 100 soles (about $25) for each participant. The trip includes transportation, admission fees, and a guide. You may book a trip online or at any travel agency in Cusco.

What to see and do: Pisac has two primary attractions: the market and the ruins. The market is conducted every day in the main center of the town, although it is notably bustling on Tuesdays, Thursdays, and Sundays. The market offers a range of handicrafts, such as alpaca wool items, silver jewelry, pottery, paintings, musical instruments, and more. You may also discover fresh fruits, vegetables, cheese, bread, and other local items. The market is an excellent place to buy souvenirs, practice your haggling abilities, and mingle with friendly traders.

The remains are on a hill above the town and part of the Ollantaytambo Archaeological Park. The ruins date back to the 15th century, and the Inca ruler Pachacuti erected them as a fortification and a religious complex. The remains include a temple, a sundial, a royal mausoleum, a wall of six monoliths, a terrace of ten niches, and a princess bath. The ruins give beautiful views of the town and the valley below and insights into Inca engineering and cosmology.

You may explore the ruins on your own or with a guide. The admission cost is 130 soles (about $32) as part of the Boleto Turistico (a ticket that includes 16 attractions in Cusco and the Sacred Valley, valid for ten days) or 70 soles (about $17) as part of the Partial Boleto Turistico (a ticket that includes four sights in the Sacred Valley, valid for two days). The ruins are accessible from 7 am to 5 pm every day.

Where to stay and eat: Pisac offers hotel alternatives for various budgets and interests. Some of the top hotels in Pisac are:

- **Pisac Inn:** This hotel is situated in the middle of the town, adjacent to the market and the church. It includes 11 pleasant rooms with private bathrooms, Wi-Fi, cable TV, heating, and balconies. It also boasts a restaurant serving organic cuisine from its garden, a bar providing live music and cultural events, and a spa offering massages and treatments. The hotel's rating is 4.5 out of 5 stars. The costs vary from $80 to $120 per night, depending on the season and the kind of hotel.

- **Melissa Wasi:** This hotel is in a calm place outside the town, surrounded by nature and mountains. It features 12 large rooms with private bathrooms, Wi-

Fi, cable TV, heating, and patios. It also boasts a restaurant providing world cuisine with local ingredients, a garden with hammocks and fire pits, and a library with books and games. The hotel has a rating of 4 star. The costs vary from $60 to $100 per night, depending on the season and the kind of accommodation.

- **Hospedaje Familiar Kitamayu:** This hotel is situated near the bus station in the town center. It features ten modest rooms with private bathrooms, Wi-Fi, cable TV, heating, and fans. It also features a common kitchen visitors may use to create their meals, a laundry service that costs by weight, and a tour desk to organize tours and activities. The hotel has a rating of 3.5 stars. The costs vary from $20 to $40 per night, depending on the season and the accommodation style.

Pisac also features a range of restaurants and cafés that appeal to varied interests and budgets. Some of the greatest places to eat in Pisac are:

- **Ulrike's café:** This café is situated in the main center of the town, and it is a popular destination for breakfast and lunch. It provides great coffee, fresh juices, sandwiches, salads, soups, pizzas, pasta, and desserts. It also includes vegetarian, vegan, and gluten-free alternatives. The café is open from 7 am to 6 pm every day. The costs vary from 10 to 30 soles (approximately $2.5 to $7.5) per dish.

- **Mullu:** This restaurant is situated between the market and the church and is a fantastic spot for supper. It provides fusion food that incorporates Peruvian, Asian, and Mediterranean ingredients. It also features a bar that sells cocktails, wines, and beers. The restaurant is open from 6 pm to 10 pm every day. The rates vary from 20 to 50 soles (approximately $5 to $12.5) per dish.

- **Cuchara de Palo:** This restaurant is situated between the bus station and the bridge, and it is an excellent spot for lunch or supper. It provides typical Peruvian food, such as ceviche, lomo saltado, quinoa soup, fish, alpaca, and cuy (guinea pig). It also provides a buffet option that includes salad, soup, main meal, dessert, and drink. The restaurant is open from 11 am to 9 pm every day. The costs vary from 15 to 40 soles (approximately $3.75 to $10) per dish.

Pisac is a vibrant market and a hilltop stronghold that provides lots of things to do and see for those who wish to experience the real and traditional side of Peru and appreciate the magnificent grandeur of the Andes.

CHAPTER 6

3-6 Days Itinerary for Machu Picchu

Machu Picchu is one of the world's most renowned and awe-inspiring sites. The historic Inca citadel, positioned on a steep slope above the Urubamba River, is a tribute to the creativity and skill of the people who constructed it more than 500 years ago. Whether you want to explore the site in detail, walk the surrounding trails, or immerse yourself in the culture and history of the area, this Itinerary will help you plan your ideal vacation to Machu Picchu.

Day 1: Arrival in Cusco

Cusco is the entrance to Machu Picchu and the Sacred Valley and a fascinating city in its own right. The historic capital of the Inca Empire, Cusco offers a combination of colonial and indigenous architecture, culture, and cuisine. Your first day may be spent adjusting to the altitude (Cusco is 3,400 meters or 11,200 feet above sea level) and exploring the city's landmarks. You could see the following attractions:

- The Plaza de Armas, the main plaza of Cusco, is surrounded by gorgeous cathedrals, museums, and stores.
- The Cathedral of Cusco, a spectacular specimen of baroque art and architecture, was constructed on the ruins of an Inca palace.

- The Qorikancha, or Temple of the Sun, the most significant sacred site of the Incas, is now partially covered by a Dominican monastery.

- The San Pedro Market is a bustling and colorful location where you can purchase anything from fresh fruits and vegetables to souvenirs and handicrafts.

- The San Blas district is lovely, with art galleries, cafés, and shops.

Where to stay: Cusco has many housing choices, ranging from inexpensive hostels to luxury hotels. Some of the nicest locations to stay are:

- Palacio del Inka, a Luxury Collection Hotel, is a five-star hotel in a historic palace near the Qorikancha. The hotel has luxury rooms, a spa, a restaurant, and a bar.

- El Mercado is a four-star hotel near the Plaza de Armas in a former market. The hotel has pleasant rooms, a courtyard, a restaurant, and a bar.

- Niños Hotel is a three-star hotel built in a colonial structure near the San Pedro Market. The hotel has basic rooms, a garden, a restaurant, and a bar. The hotel also sponsors a nonprofit that aids local youngsters.

Where to eat: Cusco provides various alternatives, from traditional Peruvian cuisine to foreign specialties. Some of the greatest places to eat are:

- Chicha, a restaurant founded by famous chef Gastón Acurio, delivers inventive and tasty meals produced with local products.

- Cicciolina, a restaurant in the San Blas area, serves Mediterranean-inspired meals with a Peruvian touch.

- Pachapapa, a restaurant in the San Blas district, offers rustic and substantial cuisine cooked in a wood-fired oven or on a grill.

Day 2: Sacred Valley Tour

The Sacred Valley is a lush and picturesque valley from Pisac to Ollantaytambo along the Urubamba River. The valley was an important agricultural and spiritual center for the Incas, home to numerous spectacular ruins, marketplaces, and settlements. You can take a full-day excursion from Cusco to view some of the attractions in the valley. Some of the locations you may visit are:

Pisac is a town famed for its colorful market and spectacular ruins on top of a hill. You may stroll among the booths offering handicrafts, textiles, and jewelry and then trek to the ruins to see the vistas and terraces.

Moray is an archaeological site composed of circular terraces that resemble a theater. The Incas utilized the terraces as an agricultural laboratory to experiment with various crops and microclimates.

Maras a town famed for its salt mines that date back to pre-Inca times. The salt mines comprise hundreds of ponds filled with salty water from a natural spring. The water evaporates and leaves behind white crystals that are gathered by hand.

Ollantaytambo is a town that keeps its ancient Inca layout and architecture. You may tour the small alleyways and stone structures and then visit the stronghold that overlooks the town. The castle was one of the final strongholds of the Incas against the Spanish invaders.

Where to stay: You may either return to Cusco or stay overnight in Ollantaytambo. If you opt to stay in Ollantaytambo, some of the greatest locations to stay are:

- El Albergue Ollantaytambo is a four-star hotel at the railway station in Ollantaytambo. The hotel has lovely rooms, a garden, a restaurant, and a bar.

- Sol Ollantay Hotel is a three-star hotel situated in the middle of Ollantaytambo. The hotel has pleasant rooms, a balcony, a restaurant, and a bar.

- Mama Simona Ollantaytambo is a two-star hostel situated on the outskirts of Ollantaytambo. The hostel has pleasant rooms, a common space, a kitchen, and a garden.

Where to eat: Ollantaytambo provides several wonderful eating alternatives, from local delicacies to international food. Some of the greatest places to eat are:

- El Albergue Restaurant, a restaurant in the El Albergue Ollantaytambo hotel, provides organic and seasonal meals produced from their farm and garden products.

- Apu Veronica, a restaurant in the middle of Ollantaytambo, provides traditional and fusion meals emphasizing Andean tastes and ingredients.

- Hearts Cafe, a cafe in the middle of Ollantaytambo, offers healthy and delicious food, snacks, and beverages. The café also supports a social initiative that aids rural people in the valley.

Day 3: Machu Picchu

Machu Picchu is the pinnacle of every journey to Peru and one of the most spectacular sights you will ever visit. The old fortress, erected by the Incas in the 15th century, is surrounded by beautiful mountains and clouds, creating a magnificent and mystical environment.

You may visit Machu Picchu by taking a train from Ollantaytambo or Cusco to Aguas Calientes, the town at the foot of the monument, and then taking a bus or trekking up to the entrance. You may also trek the Inca Trail or other alternate routes to Machu Picchu, but you must schedule them well in advance and have more time. Some of the things you may see and do in Machu Picchu are:

- Explore the key sections of the site, such as the Temple of the Sun, the Intihuatana stone, the Temple of the Three Windows, and the Temple of the Condor.
- Hike up to Huayna Picchu or Machu Picchu Mountain, two peaks that give amazing views of the monument and the valley. You will need to acquire individual tickets for these treks and reserve them in advance since they have limited availability.

- Visit the Sun Gate or the Inca Bridge, two places part of the Inca Trail and give various vistas of Machu Picchu. You don't need additional tickets for these treks, although they might be tough and take some time.

- Learn more about the history and culture of Machu Picchu by hiring a tour or downloading an audio guide app on your phone. You will also discover informational signs and maps around the property.

Where to stay: You may either return to Cusco or Ollantaytambo or stay overnight in Aguas Calientes. If you opt to stay in Aguas Calientes, some of the greatest locations to stay are:

- Inkaterra Machu Picchu Pueblo Hotel is a five-star hotel in a natural reserve near Aguas Calientes. The hotel has elegant rooms, a spa, a restaurant, and a bar.

- Tierra Viva Machu Picchu is a four-star hotel in Aguas Calientes. The hotel has contemporary rooms, a patio, a breakfast area, and a lounge.

- Eco Quechua Lodge is a three-star hotel in Mandor Valley near Aguas Calientes. The hotel has rustic rooms, a garden, a restaurant, and a bar.

Where to eat: Aguas Calientes provides several great alternatives, from pizza and spaghetti to quinoa and alpaca. Some of the greatest places to eat are:

- Indio Feliz, a restaurant in the middle of Aguas Calientes, provides French and Peruvian meals with ample amounts and imaginative presentations.

- Tree House Restaurant & Cafe, a restaurant in the middle of Aguas Calientes, provides fusion meals with Asian and Mediterranean influences.

- La Boulangerie de Paris, a bakery in the middle of Aguas Calientes, sells fresh bread, pastries, sandwiches, and coffee.

Day 4: Transfer to Cusco

You may spend your fourth day commuting back to Cusco by train, bus, or cab. You may also use your time in Aguas Calientes by seeing some of its attractions before departing. Some of the things you can see and do in Aguas Calientes are:

- Relax in the hot springs that give the town its name.

- Visit the Manuel Chávez Ballón Site Museum, which showcases artifacts and information concerning Machu Picchu and its discovery.

- Visit the Butterfly House, a facility that highlights the richness and beauty of the butterflies that reside in the area.

- Visit the Orchid Garden, a spot that shows the diversity and grandeur of the nearby orchids.

- Once you arrive in Cusco, you may spend the remainder of the day at your leisure. You may rest at your hotel, go shopping, or join a nightlife tour.

Day 5: Cusco Free Day

You may spend your fifth day in Cusco how you like. You may take it easy and enjoy the city's beauty and atmosphere or join an optional excursion to explore some neighboring sights. Some of the excursions you may pick from are:

- A half-day journey to Sacsayhuaman, Qenko, Puca Pucara, and Tambomachay, four ancient sites situated on the outskirts of Cusco. These sites were part of the Inca defensive system and ceremonial complex, and they display the outstanding engineering and architecture of the Incas.

- A full-day journey to Rainbow Mountain, a natural beauty that boasts multicolored stripes of minerals on its slopes. The trek to Rainbow Mountain is tough but rewarding, as you will encounter spectacular landscapes and animals.

- A full-day journey to Humantay Lake, a turquoise lagoon nestled at the foot of a snow-capped mountain. The climb to Humantay Lake is modest yet spectacular, as you will travel through valleys, rivers, and glaciers.

Where to stay: You might remain in the same hotel as previously or select a new one. See Day 1 for some suggestions.

Where to dine: You may eat at the same restaurants as previously or try some new ones. See Day 1 for some options.

Day 6: Departure from Cusco

Depending on your travel itinerary, you may spend your final day in Cusco. You may either rest at your hotel, do some last-minute shopping, or explore some of the sights you missed previously. Some of the locations you may visit are:

- The San Francisco Church and Convent is a colonial complex that comprises a church, a convent, a museum, and a library. The church boasts a gorgeous front and interior, while the convent contains a collection of paintings, sculptures, and relics. The museum shows religious art and relics, while the library has many old texts.

- The Museum of Pre-Columbian Art is a museum that displays art and items from numerous pre-Columbian civilizations that occupied Peru. The museum includes a range of artifacts, such as pottery, textiles, metalwork, and jewelry.

- The Chocolate Museum is a museum that highlights the history and culture of chocolate in Peru. The museum features interactive exhibitions, seminars, and tastings.

- When departing, you may take a cab or a shuttle to the airport and catch your journey back home. You will have memorable memories and experiences during your journey to Machu Picchu.

This chapter offers guidance on how to spend 3-7 days at Machu Picchu and its surroundings. It covers the following topics:

- **Arrival in Cusco:** How to travel to Cusco from Lima or other places in Peru, and what to see and do on your first day.

- **Sacred Valley trip:** How to take a full-day trip from Cusco to see some of the wonders of the Sacred

Valley, such as Pisac, Moray, Maras, and Ollantaytambo.

- **Machu Picchu:** How to travel to Machu Picchu from Ollantaytambo or Cusco by rail or hike, and what to see and do at the site.

- **Transfer to Cusco:** How to return to Cusco by train, bus, or cab, and what to see and do in Aguas Calientes before departing.

- **Cusco Free Day:** How to spend your free day in Cusco as you choose, or take an extra excursion to explore some local sights.

- **Departure from Cusco:** How to spend your final day in Cusco, depending on your departure schedule, and how to get to the airport.

We have reached the culmination of the 3-7 days itinerary for Machu Picchu. We hope you liked this chapter and found it beneficial for your vacation planning. You have learned how to travel to Cusco, the entrance to Machu Picchu and the Sacred Valley, and what to see and do in this interesting city. This proposed Itinerary will enable you to explore Machu Picchu with a wonderful approach.

CHAPTER 7: Travel Tips

When is the ideal time to visit Machu Picchu?

Machu Picchu is a year-round attraction, but there are several elements to consider when organizing your journey. The key considerations are the weather, the people, and the availability of permits and tickets.

Weather

Machu Picchu has two seasons: the dry season (May to September) and the rainy season (October to April). Bright skies, sunny days, and cold nights characterize the dry season. The average temperature is approximately 20°C (68°F) during the day and 8°C (46°F) at night. Frequent rains, gloomy skies, and humid weather characterize the rainy season. The average temperature is roughly 18°C (64°F) during the day and 12°C (54°F) at night.

The dry season is often considered the ideal time to visit Machu Picchu since you'll get greater views of the ruins and the surrounding mountains. However, this also implies that this is the peak season, with more visitors and higher rates. The wet season has its perks too, since you'll discover fewer people, reduced pricing, and more greenery. The rain normally falls in the afternoon, so you may still enjoy some bright hours in the morning. However, you'll also have to cope with mud, treacherous paths, and landslides.

Crowds

Machu Picchu is one of the most famous sites in Peru, and it may become extremely busy during the peak season. The busiest months are June, July, and August, when hundreds of tourists throng the site daily. You'll have to buy your tickets and permits well in advance since they sell out rapidly. You'll also have to contend with lengthy queues, packed buses, and limited space on the hikes and at the vistas.

The low season runs from September through May, when there are fewer tourists and greater availability of tickets and permits. You'll have more flexibility and freedom to browse the site at your speed. You'll also have more opportunities to mingle with people and explore their culture.

Permits and tickets

Machu Picchu has a restricted capacity of 2,500 people daily, and you require a ticket to access the monument. You may purchase your ticket online or at authorized Cusco or Aguas Calientes offices. There are many sorts of tickets available, depending on what you want to see and do at Machu Picchu:

Machu Picchu Only: This ticket enables you to enter the major archaeological site of Machu Picchu. You may select between two-time slots: 6 am to 12 pm or 12 pm to 5:30 pm. The fee is 152 soles (about $45) for adults and 77 soles (about $23) for students.

Machu Picchu + Huayna Picchu: This ticket enables you to enter both the major archaeological site of Machu Picchu and Huayna Picchu mountain, which gives breathtaking views of the citadel from above. You may select between two slots: from 6 am to 10 am or 10 am to 2 pm. The fee is 200 soles (about $59) for adults and 125 soles (about $37) for students.

Machu Picchu + Machu Picchu Mountain: This ticket enables you to enter the major archaeological site of Machu

Picchu and the Machu Picchu mountain, which is higher than Huayna Picchu and gives panoramic views of the valley. You may select between two slots: from 6 am to 10 am or 10 am to 2 pm. The fee is 200 soles (about $59) for adults and 125 soles (about $37) for students.

Machu Picchu + Museum: This ticket enables you to enter the major archaeological site of Machu Picchu and the Manuel Chávez Ballón Site Museum, which exhibits artifacts and information about the history and culture of Machu Picchu. You may select any time between 6 am and 5:30 pm. The fee is 174 soles (about $51) for adults and 99 soles (about $29) for students.

If you wish to trek the Inca Trail to Machu Picchu, you need a permit and your ticket. The Inca Trail has a restricted capacity of 500 people daily, including guides and porters. You need to arrange your permit from a qualified tour operator at least six months in advance since they sell out rapidly. The price of the permit varies based on the duration and complexity of the journey, but it normally runs from $600 to $900 per person.

Conclusion

There is no precise answer to the ideal time to visit Machu Picchu since it depends on your unique interests and expectations. However, here are some broad suggestions based on the issues stated above:

- To experience the greatest weather and vistas, visit Machu Picchu during the dry season (May to September). However, be prepared to encounter greater people and more rates.

- If you want to escape the crowds and save some money, visit Machu Picchu during the rainy season (October to April). However, be prepared to cope with rain and muck.

- If you wish to trek the Inca Trail to Machu Picchu, book your permit well in advance and find a reliable tour company. The ideal months to trek the Inca Trail are May and September since they balance weather and tourists.

- You'll be astounded by its beauty and mystery whenever you visit Machu Picchu. Machu Picchu is a site that will remain in your memories forever.

What to take for your vacation to Machu Picchu

Machu Picchu is a bucket-list destination for many tourists, but getting there requires careful planning and preparation. Whether you want to climb the Inca Trail, ride the train, or join a tour, you must prepare intelligently for your journey to the ancient citadel. Here are some recommendations on what to pack and what to leave behind.

Clothing: Machu Picchu has a subtropical highland climate, which may be warm and humid during the day but chilly and dry at night. The weather may also vary abruptly, particularly during the rainy season from November to March. Therefore, it is essential to bring layers of clothes that may be quickly added or withdrawn as required. Some vital elements are:

- A waterproof jacket or poncho to protect you from rain and wind.

- A fleece or sweatshirt for cold nights and mornings.
- A hat, sunglasses, and sunscreen to shelter you from the sun's rays.
- A scarf or buff to protect your lips and nose in case of dust or pollution.

- Comfortable hiking shoes or boots with strong grip and support.
- Breathable socks and underwear that can be washed and dried fast.
- Lightweight trousers and shirts that are moisture-wicking and quick-drying.
- A swimsuit if you wish to visit the hot springs in Aguas Calientes.

Papers: You must always carry several crucial papers with you throughout your journey to Machu Picchu. These include:

1. Your passport must be valid for at least six months from your date of entrance into Peru. You will also need a photocopy of your passport if you lose it or must present it to authorities.

2. Your Machu Picchu ticket, which must be bought in advance online or via an approved agent. You must present your ticket and passport at the access gate. You may print your ticket or display it on your phone, but ensure you have adequate juice and signal.

3. Your Covid-19 immunization certificate or negative PCR test result is necessary for accessing Machu Picchu as of March 18, 2022. You will also need to wear two surgical face masks within the sanctuary.

4. Your train or bus ticket if you are not trekking to Machu Picchu. You must present your ticket and passport at the station or the bus stop. You may print your ticket or display it on your phone, but again, ensure you have adequate juice and connectivity.

5. Your travel insurance coverage should cover medical bills, emergency evacuation, theft, loss, and cancellation. You never know what can happen during your journey. Therefore, it is best to be cautious than sorry.

Gear: Depending on how you want to go to Machu Picchu, you may need extra gear to make your trip more comfortable and pleasurable. Some helpful products are:

1. A backpack or daypack that can accommodate all your things and is simple to carry. If you are hiking the Inca Trail or on another multi-day journey, you may wish to hire a porter or a mule to carry your heavy gear and bring a small backpack with your necessities.

2. A reusable water container that can be replenished at specific spots along the journey. Tap water in Peru is not safe to drink. Therefore, you must purchase bottled water or purify it using pills or filters.

3. A camera or phone with adequate capacity and battery to record the beautiful sights of Machu Picchu and its surroundings. You can also pack a power bank, a charger, and an adaptor for Peru's outlets (type A or C).

4. A torch or headlamp for trekking in the dark or exploring the place after sunset. Machu Picchu does not have artificial lighting. Therefore, you will need your source of illumination.

5. A first aid package includes basic items such as bandages, antiseptic wipes, painkillers, anti-diarrhea tablets, bug repellent, and altitude sickness medicine. Machu Picchu is positioned at 2,430 meters (7,970 feet) above sea level, which may produce headaches, nausea, dizziness, and shortness of breath in certain individuals.

Extras: There are some extra goods that you may wish to carry for your journey to Machu Picchu based on your specific tastes and requirements. Some possibilities are:

1. A book or a handbook on Machu Picchu's history, culture, and architecture. You may also download an audio tour app for further information and insights.

2. A pair of binoculars or a telescope for seeing animals and features of the place. Machu Picchu is home to

various birds, animals, reptiles, and plants worth seeing.

3. A diary or a sketchbook for capturing your thoughts and experiences. Machu Picchu is a site of inspiration and awe, and you may wish to convey your emotions and ideas in words or photographs.

4. A snack or a dessert to reward oneself after reaching the spot. Pack some coca leaves or candies to chew on for energy and altitude relief.

5. A keepsake or a present for yourself or your loved ones. You may discover numerous handicrafts and goods manufactured by local craftsmen in the marketplaces and stores surrounding Machu Picchu, such as textiles, pottery, jewelry, and chocolate.

How to acquire your Machu Picchu admission ticket?

Machu Picchu is one of the world's most renowned and awe-inspiring sites. The ancient Inca fortress, positioned on a rocky crest above the Sacred Valley, is a UNESCO World Heritage Site and a miracle of engineering and construction. To visit this gorgeous destination, you must purchase your Machu Picchu admission ticket in advance since the number of tourists is restricted to 4000 daily. Here are some tips on how to acquire your ticket for the 2023-2024 season.

Many sorts of tickets are available for Machu Picchu, based on what you want to see and do. The most frequent ticket is the Machu Picchu Standard Admission Ticket, which offers admission to the major archaeological site and four circuits to explore it. You may select the time of your admission, from 6 am to 2 pm, and you have up to four hours to visit the site. This ticket costs $58 for adults, $32 for children, and $39 for students with a valid ISIC card.

If you are ambitious and wish to trek one of the two mountains bordering Machu Picchu, you may select the

Huayna Picchu trek Permit or the Machu Picchu Mountain Hike Permit. These tickets include the basic entrance to the attraction plus access to one of the mountains. Huayna Picchu is the smaller and steeper peak, affording amazing views of the citadel and the surrounding valley. Machu Picchu Peak is the bigger and taller peak, affording panoramic views of the whole region. Both treks are demanding and need a decent degree of fitness and acclimatization. The Huayna Picchu Hike Permit is $70 for adults, $45 for children, and $57 for students. The Machu Picchu Mountain Hike Permit is $65 for adults, $40 for children, and $52 for students. There are two-time windows for each hike: 7 am or 10 am for Huayna Picchu and 6 am or 9 am for Machu Picchu Mountain.

To receive your Machu Picchu admission ticket, you need to book it online via an approved website or agency. You cannot purchase tickets at the entrance to the facility. The official website of the Ministry of Culture of Peru is [Machupicchu.gob.pe], where you can check availability and rates and make reservations. However, this website could be more user-friendly and may have technical faults or glitches. Another alternative is to purchase via a trustworthy

partner website such as [Machu-picchu.org] or [Machupicchugob.pe], which provide:
- A hassle-free booking procedure.
- Real-time availability.
- Timely ticket delivery.
- Customer assistance.
- Secure online payment.
- Group booking possibilities.

These websites also provide extra services such as guided tours, rail tickets, bus tickets, hotels, and packages.

To reserve your ticket online, you need to complete these steps:

- Choose the sort of ticket you want: basic entry, Huayna Picchu trek permit, or Machu Picchu Mountain hike permit.

- Choose the day and time of your visit. Check the availability of tickets on the calendar.

- Fill up your personal information: name, passport number, nationality, age, etc. Make sure that your information corresponds perfectly with your passport or ID card.

- Make the payment using your credit card or PayPal account. You will get a confirmation email with your reservation number.

- Print your ticket or download it to your mobile device. You must display it with your genuine passport or ID card at the door.

Some suggestions to bear in mind while reserving your ticket are:

- Book your ticket as early as possible, particularly if you plan to trek Huayna Picchu or Machu Picchu Mountain since these tickets sell out rapidly.

- Be flexible with your dates and times since your selection may not be available.

- Check the weather prediction before reserving your ticket since Machu Picchu may be closed due to excessive rain or landslides.

- Please read carefully the terms and conditions of your ticket since no returns or modifications are permitted after you book it.

- Plan carefully how you will go to Machu Picchu from Cusco or Ollantaytambo. You may take a train to Aguas Calientes (the closest town) and then a bus or walk to the site entrance. Alternatively, you may trek the Inca Trail or other ways that lead to Machu Picchu.

- Getting your Machu Picchu admission ticket is crucial to visit this beautiful destination. By following this instruction, you can secure your seat and have one of the most remarkable moments of your life.

How to be a careful traveler?

Machu Picchu is not simply a UNESCO World Legacy Site but a spiritual location for the locals and a symbol of Peru's rich cultural legacy. As a tourist, you have the chance to see this marvel of the world, but also the obligation to respect and safeguard it. Here are some recommendations on how to be a safe visitor while visiting Machu Picchu:

Respect the rules and regulations.

Machu Picchu has tight restrictions and procedures to safeguard its integrity and avoid harm. As a responsible tourist, you should follow them and respect the advice of the personnel and guides. Some of the regulations are:

1. Do not touch, climb, or sit on the walls or buildings.
2. Do not trash or leave any sign of your stay.
3. Do not bring any food, beverages (except water), or plastic bottles.
4. Do not smoke or ignite any fire.
5. Do not use drones, tripods, selfie sticks, or flash photography.
6. Do not make loud sounds or play music.

7. Do not feed or disturb the animals.
8. Support the local community.

One of the finest ways to be a responsible tourist is to assist the local communities of the areas you visit. By purchasing and dining locally, you are helping families and small businesses in the region while also experiencing genuine goods and food. Some of the methods to help the local community are:

1. Buy souvenirs from local artisans and marketplaces, such as handicrafts, textiles, pottery, or jewelry.
2. Eat at local restaurants or food vendors, where you may experience excellent meals like ceviche, quinoa soup, or cuy (guinea pig).
3. Hire a local guide or join a community-based tour, where you may learn more about the history and culture of Machu Picchu and its surroundings.
4. Tip liberally for excellent service, and don't negotiate too hard for a reasonable price.
5. Be careful of your influence.

Machu Picchu is a vulnerable ecology impacted by climate change, pollution, and over-tourism. As a responsible traveler, you should be conscious of your influence on the environment and attempt to limit it as much as possible. Some of the methods to be conscious of your effect are:

1. Choose sustainable lodging and travel companies with environmental and social policies and practices.
2. Reduce your carbon footprint by utilizing public transit, walking, or cycling wherever feasible.
3. Minimize your waste by carrying reusable bags, bottles, and containers and correctly recycling or disposing the waste.
4. Conserve water and energy by taking short showers, shutting off lights and appliances when unused, and utilizing solar chargers or batteries for your electronics.

Learn about the culture and history.

Machu Picchu is a spectacular archaeological monument and a living witness of the Inca culture and its history. As a responsible visitor, you should learn about the culture and history of Machu Picchu and its people and respect their variety and richness. Some of the methods to learn about the culture and history are:

1. Visit the Manuel Chávez Ballón Site Museum to examine relics and information concerning Machu Picchu's discovery, construction, and use.
2. Explore the numerous districts and buildings of Machu Picchu, such as the Temple of the Sun, the Intihuatana Stone, and the Royal Tomb.
3. Experience the Inti Raymi celebration, held every June 24 in Cusco, and commemorates the Inca sun deity with music, dances, and ceremonies.
4. Respect the local customs and traditions, such as dressing modestly, asking for permission before taking photographs, or providing a gift or money to religious locations.

Have fun and enjoy

Machu Picchu is a once-in-a-lifetime location that will leave you breathless and stunned. As a responsible tourist, you should have fun and enjoy your vacation, but also remember that you are a guest in someone else's house. Some of the methods to have fun and pleasure are:

1. Be adaptable and open-minded to new experiences and challenges.
2. Be kind and respectful to other visitors and residents.
3. Be interested and ask inquiries to learn more about Machu Picchu and Peru.
4. Be glad and appreciative of the chance to visit Machu Picchu.

Being a responsible tourist while visiting Machu Picchu involves respecting and safeguarding this beautiful place and its inhabitants while still having fun and enjoying your vacation. By following the advice in this chapter, you will not only have a wonderful and satisfying experience but also contribute to the preservation and sustainability of Machu Picchu for future generations.

Visa Requirements for Machu Picchu

Machu Picchu is one of South America's most famous and awe-inspiring locations and a must-see for any tourist who wishes to study the ancient Inca civilization. However, before you pack your bags and book your flights, you must be sure you have the necessary visa to enter Peru to visit this UNESCO World Heritage site.

Do I need a visa to visit Peru?

The answer depends on your nationality and the purpose and length of your stay. Peru provides a visa exemption policy for nationals of numerous countries who may visit Peru for leisure or business reasons without a visa for up to 183 days each year. Some of the nations that are visa-exempt for Peru include:

- Argentina
- Australia
- Brazil
- Canada
- Chile
- Colombia
- Ecuador

- France
- Germany
- Italy
- Japan
- Mexico
- Netherlands
- New Zealand
- Singapore
- Spain
- United Kingdom
- United States

You may check the list of visa-exempt countries and the maximum stay permitted for each one on the Peruvian Ministry of Foreign Affairs official website. If your nation is missing from the list, you must apply for a tourist or business visa at the closest Peruvian consulate or embassy before traveling.

What documents do I need to enter Peru?

Whether you require a visa or not, you will need to provide the following papers when you arrive in Peru:

1. A valid passport with at least six months of validity from the entrance date.
2. A return, onward ticket, or evidence of adequate finances to cover your stay.
3. A completed immigration form (Tarjeta Andina de Migración) that you will get on the aircraft or at the border.
4. You will need to complete a health declaration form (Declaración Jurado de Salud) online before your arrival as part of the COVID-19 preventative efforts.

You may also be requested to present evidence of lodging, trip itinerary, health insurance, or immunization certificates, depending on the current requirements and the judgment of the immigration officer. It is suggested to check the latest travel information and regulations on the official website of the Peruvian Ministry of Foreign Affairs or contact your local Peruvian consulate or embassy before your trip.

How can I receive tickets and permits to visit Machu Picchu?

Once you have gotten your visa and entrance documentation, you must purchase tickets and permits to visit Machu Picchu. Due to its popularity and conservation efforts, Machu Picchu has a restricted number of visitors daily and per session. To prevent disappointment, you must buy your tickets and permits in advance, preferably online.

Many tickets and permits are available for Machu Picchu, depending on what you want to see and do. The primary possibilities are:

Machu Picchu Only: This ticket enables you to access and tour the main citadel of Machu Picchu, following one of the three circuits offered. You may select from eight session times, from 6 am to 2 pm, and remain for up to four hours. The price is 152 soles (about $38) for adults, 77 soles (about $19) for students, and 70 soles (about $18) for children.

Machu Picchu + Huayna Picchu: This ticket enables you to access and tour the main citadel of Machu Picchu, following circuit #3, and also trek up to the peak of Huayna Picchu, the famous mountain that overlooks the site. You may select from three different session times, from 6 am to 9 am, and remain for up to four hours. The fee is 200 soles (about $50) for adults, 125 soles (about $31) for students, and 118 soles (about $30) for children.

Machu Picchu + Machu Picchu Mountain: This ticket enables you to access and tour the main citadel of Machu Picchu, following circuit #3, and also trek up to the top of Machu Picchu Mountain, another mountain that gives panoramic views of the site. You may select from four different session times, from 6 am to 11 am, and remain for up to four hours. The fee is 200 soles (about $50) for adults, 125 soles (about $31) for students, and 118 soles (about $30) for children.

You may order your tickets and permits online on the official website of the Peruvian Ministry of Culture or via a certified tour operator or travel agency. You must give your passport data and choose your date and session time. You will also need to pay online with a credit or debit card or via other payment options accessible. You will get a confirmation email with a QR code that you will need to print or present on your phone when you enter Machu Picchu.

What else do I need to know before visiting Machu Picchu?

Besides receiving your visa and tickets, there are several additional things you need to know and prepare before visiting Machu Picchu. Here are some hints and recommendations:

You must carry your passport to Machu Picchu since it is essential for identification and security reasons. You may also acquire a unique stamp on your passport at the gate to remember your stay.

You will need to visit Machu Picchu with a professional tour guide, who can explain the history and importance of the place and assist you in obeying the laws and restrictions. You may hire a guide at the entry or arrange one in advance via a tour operator or travel agency.

You will need to follow the allocated circuit and session time that you have booked and heed the signs and directions of the personnel and guards. You cannot backtrack, change circuits, or remain longer than your authorized time. You are also prohibited from bringing food, beverages (except water), umbrellas, tripods, drones, or other objects that may harm or disrupt the site.

Considering the weather and the altitude, you will need to dress correctly and comfortably for your visit. Machu Picchu is 2,430 meters (7,970 feet) above sea level and has a subtropical climate, with warm days and cool nights. You should wear layers of clothes, sunscreen, sunglasses, a hat, and sturdy shoes. You should also carry a raincoat or poncho, particularly during the rainy season from November to March.

You must care for your health and safety throughout your vacation, particularly if you suffer from altitude sickness or other medical concerns. You should drink lots of water, avoid alcohol and caffeine, eat light meals, and rest well before and after your appointment. You should also have travel insurance that covers emergency evacuation and medical expenditures in case of an accident or sickness.

Conclusion

Visiting Machu Picchu is a once-in-a-lifetime adventure that demands some planning and preparation. Following this advice, you can ensure you have the necessary visa, documentation, tickets, and permissions to visit Peru and enjoy this beautiful place. You may also discover some important ideas and advice to make the most of your stay and enjoy it safely and responsibly.

Custom and Etiquette

Machu Picchu is not just a spectacular archaeological site but also a spiritual location for the local people and the ancestors of the Incas. To visit this amazing location, you need to respect its cultural and ecological legacy and the norms and regulations that strive to protect it. Here is some advice on how to act in Machu Picchu, respecting the traditions and etiquette of the area.

- Refrain from carrying food or beverages into Machu Picchu. There is a strict regulation of no food or beverages inside the site, save for water. You may leave your food and beverages outside the entry gates, where lockers and eateries are accessible. This is to safeguard the site and the fauna from rubbish and pollution.

- Do remain on the defined paths and obey the signage. Machu Picchu is a delicate old monument that must be safeguarded from erosion and harm. Wandering off the pathways might injure the ruins and risk oneself since high cliffs and tumbling boulders exist. There are four circuits to tour the site, each with differing degrees of effort and time.

- Do not get nude or pose improperly. Machu Picchu is a holy destination for many people, and you should respect its spiritual importance. Getting nude or making obscene gestures is not only impolite but also unlawful. You might be punished or ejected from the site if you do so.

- Do respect the llamas and other animals. Machu Picchu is home to numerous llamas, alpacas, birds, and other wildlife that graze freely about the site. They are part of the natural and cultural legacy of the area, and you should not disturb or feed them. You may snap photographs of them from a safe distance but do not touch them or pursue them.

- Remember to underestimate the effort of walking to Machu Picchu. If you go to Machu Picchu by the Inca Trail or other ways, you must be prepared for the physical effort and the high altitude. The Inca Trail is a four-day hike that covers numerous passes over

4,000 meters high, with steep slopes and rocky terrain. You must be healthy, acclimatized, and have adequate gear and permissions to perform it. Other routes may be shorter or longer but still need excellent health and preparedness.

- Do not touch or climb on the remains. Machu Picchu is a wonder of engineering and construction that has lasted millennia. You should appreciate it from a respectful distance, without touching or climbing on the stones. This may harm the buildings and create accidents. You should also avoid using flash photography or tripods since they might damage the site or block other visitors.

- Do snap amazing shots and enjoy the vista. Machu Picchu is one of the most picturesque destinations in the world, and you should capture its splendor with your camera or phone. However, you should also take some time to enjoy it with your actual eyes, without staring at a screen. Machu Picchu is a wonderful destination that will inspire and leave you breathless.

Machu Picchu is a destination that merits your attention and adoration. By following these recommendations on traditions and etiquette, you will have a more delightful and memorable stay while contributing to its protection and appreciation.

Language and Communication

Machu Picchu is a UNESCO World Heritage Site and one of the most visited sites in South America. It is also a site where you can experience Peru's rich and varied culture, including its languages. Peru has 47 native languages. However, the most generally spoken are Spanish, Quechua, and Aymara. Spanish is the national language of Peru and the predominant language of communication in Machu Picchu. However, many people also speak Quechua, the language of the Incas who constructed the historic fortress.

Quechua is a sophisticated and beautiful language that has various dialects and variants. Some terms in Quechua have no clear equivalent in Spanish or English, such as "ayni," which denotes reciprocity or mutual help2. Aymara is another indigenous language spoken mostly in the southern highlands of Peru, near Lake Titicaca. Aymara is linked to Quechua but contains several special elements, such as reverse word order and a three-way differentiation between past, present, and future.

If you wish to converse with the natives in Machu Picchu, it is useful to learn some simple words in Spanish and

Quechua. English is generally spoken by tour guides and hotel personnel, but only by some. Learning basic Spanish and Quechua can make your vacation simpler and demonstrate respect and admiration for the local culture. Here are some important terms and phrases to get you started:

- Hello: Hola (Spanish), Rimaykullayki (Quechua)
- Goodbye: Adiós (Spanish), Tupananchiskama (Quechua)
- Thank you: Gracias (Spanish), Solpayki (Quechua)
- How are you?: ¿Cómo estás? (Spanish), Allillanchu? (Quechua)
- I'm fine: Estoy bien (Spanish), Allillanmi (Quechua)
- What is your name?: ¿Cómo te llamas? (Spanish), Iman sutiyki? (Quechua)
- My name is...: Me llamo... (Spanish), Sutiymi... (Quechua)
- Where are you from?: ¿De dónde eres? (Spanish), Maymantam kanki? (Quechua)
- I'm from...: Soy de... (Spanish), ...manta kani (Quechua)

- How much is it?: ¿Cuánto cuesta? (Spanish), Hayk'ataj? (Quechua)

- Do you speak English?: ¿Hablas inglés? (Spanish), Inlish simita rimankichu? (Quechua)
- I don't understand: No entiendo (Spanish), Mana yachani (Quechua)
- Excuse me: Perdón (Spanish), Dispinsayuway (Quechua)
- Sorry: Lo siento (Spanish), Pampachayuway (Quechua)

You may also utilize gestures and body language to communicate at Machu Picchu. For example, nodding your head says yes, shaking your head means no, lifting your eyebrows means hello or farewell, and pointing with your lips means looking over there. However, be cautious not to insult anybody with your gestures. For instance, avoid pointing with your finger since it is considered disrespectful. Also, avoid touching people's heads or caps since it is considered impolite.

Language and communication are crucial parts of every travel experience. By learning some Spanish and Quechua, you may improve your vacation to Machu Picchu and engage with the local people. You may also know more about the history and culture of Peru, which is represented in its languages. Machu Picchu is not just a spectacular archaeological monument but also a living witness of Peru's linguistic variety and vibrancy.

Health and Safety Advice

Machu Picchu is a dream destination for many people, but it also offers significant health and safety problems that you should be aware of and prepared for. Here are some ideas and recommendations to assist you in enjoying your visit to this fantastic site without any hassles.

Health

Altitude sickness is the most prevalent health risk that plagues tourists to Machu Picchu. This is caused by the low oxygen levels at high elevations, which may induce symptoms such as headache, nausea, dizziness, exhaustion, and shortness of breath. To avoid or decrease the symptoms of altitude sickness, you should:

- Acclimatize yourself gradually by spending at least two or three days in Cusco (3,400 m) or a similar high-altitude destination before heading to Machu Picchu (2,430 m).

- Drink lots of water and avoid coffee, and heavy meals.

- Chew coca leaves or drink coca tea, natural therapies that aid with altitude sickness. You may get them in local markets or pharmacies. However, be aware that coca leaves are prohibited in certain countries, so do not carry them when you leave Peru.

- Take medicine such as acetazolamide (Diamox) or ibuprofen (Advil) if you have severe symptoms or a history of altitude sickness. Consult your doctor before taking any drug, and follow the directions carefully.

- Seek medical assistance if your symptoms persist or do not improve within 24 hours. Clinics and pharmacies in Aguas Calientes (the town near Machu Picchu) and Cusco may give treatment and oxygen therapy.

Another health danger at Machu Picchu is sun exposure. The sun is powerful at high elevations and may induce sunburn, dehydration, and heatstroke. To shield oneself from the sun, you should:

- Wear sunscreen with a high SPF level and reapply it regularly.
- Wear a hat, sunglasses, and long-sleeved clothes.
- Drink lots of water.
- Seek shade and rest if you feel hot or dizzy.

A third health risk at Machu Picchu is bug bites. Mosquitoes and sandflies may spread illnesses such as malaria, dengue, yellow, and leishmaniasis. To avoid insect bites, you should:

- Use insect repellent containing DEET or picaridin and reapply it often.
- Wear long trousers and long-sleeved shirts, particularly during dawn and dusk when insects are most active.
- Sleep beneath a mosquito net or in an air-conditioned room.
- Consider taking antimalarial medicine if you go to locations where malaria is widespread. Consult your doctor before taking any drug, and follow the directions carefully.
- Gct vaccinated against yellow fever at least ten days before your trip if you are going to locations where

yellow fever is prevalent. You may need to produce evidence of immunization while entering or exiting Peru.

Safety

Machu Picchu is typically a safe site to visit, but there are several safety measures that you should follow to prevent accidents or criminality. Here are some safety recommendations for Machu Picchu:

- Follow the laws and regulations of the site, such as remaining on the identified pathways, not climbing on the walls or buildings, not feeding or touching the animals, and not littering or vandalizing the place.

- Be cautious while going on steep steps and slippery slopes, particularly when it rains. Wear sturdy shoes and, if necessary, a walking stick.

- Do not cross the ropes or obstacles that identify the prohibited zones. These regions are unsafe and off-limits for your protection.

- Only try to walk to Huayna Picchu (the peak behind Machu Picchu) or any neighboring mountains with a permit and a guide. These treks are demanding and need early scheduling and registration. See Safety Tips for Machu Picchu for further information.

- Be mindful of your surroundings and keep an eye on your stuff at all times. Make sure to leave your belongings unattended or carry big sums of cash or costly stuff. Use a padlock on your baggage while traveling by bus or rail.

- Use only official taxis or buses to go to and from Machu Picchu. Avoid hitchhiking or taking rides from strangers. Do not reveal your trip plans or personal details to someone you do not know or trust.

- Call the local authorities or your tour operator for help if you face any issues or crises. There are police stations and tourist information centers in Aguas Calientes and Cusco that might aid you.

By following these health and safety tips, you may make the most of your visit to Machu Picchu and have a wonderful and trouble-free trip. Machu Picchu is a gorgeous and interesting place that needs your attention and care.

Important Phrases to Know

Machu Picchu is not just a spectacular archaeological monument but also a cultural treasure that preserves the tradition of the Inca civilization. To truly appreciate the beauty and importance of this region, it helps to learn some basic words in the languages spoken by the local people and the ancient residents. In this chapter, you will discover several helpful terms in Spanish and Quechua, the two most frequent languages in the area, as well as some instructions on pronouncing and applying them.

Spanish Phrases

Spanish is the official language of Peru and the most frequently spoken one in the nation. It is also the language most visitors and travelers use to converse with locals and guides. However, Spanish in Peru has certain differences and influences from indigenous languages, notably in pronunciation, vocabulary, and grammar. Here are some typical Spanish words that you may need or hear during your visit to Machu Picchu:

- Hola - Hello
- Buenos días - Good morning

- Buenas tardes - Good afternoon.
- Buenas noches - Good evening / Good night
- ¿Cómo te llamas? - What is your name?
- Me llamo ... - My name is ...
- Mucho gusto - Nice to meet you
- ¿De dónde eres? - Where are you from?
- Soy de ... - I am from ...
- ¿Hablas inglés? - Do you speak English?
- No hablo español - I do not speak Spanish
- ¿Puedes hablar más despacio? - Can you talk more slowly?
- No entiendo - I do not comprehend
- ¿Qué significa ...? - What does ... mean?
- ¿Cómo se dice ... en español? - How do you say ... in Spanish?
- Gracias: Thank you.
- De nada - You are welcome
- Por favor - Please
- Disculpa or Perdón - Excuse me or Sorry
- Lo siento - I am sorry.
- Sí - Yes
- No - No

- Tal vez or Quizás - Maybe or Perhaps
- ¿Dónde está …? - Where is …?
- ¿Cómo llego a …? - How do I go there …?
- ¿Cuánto cuesta …? - How much does … cost?
- Quiero … - I desire …
- Necesito … - I need …
- Tengo … - I have …
- Me gusta … - I enjoy …
- No me gusta … - I do not like …
- Está bien or Vale: It is alright or Alright.
- ¡Salud! - Cheers! or Bless you!
- ¡Buen provecho! - Enjoy your food!
- ¡Buen viaje! - Have a pleasant vacation!
- ¡Adiós! or ¡Chau! - Goodbye!
- Some advice on how to pronounce Spanish words are:
- The letter h is silent, e.g., hola is pronounced as ola.
- The letter j sounds like h in English, e.g., jamón is pronounced as hamón.
- The letter ll sounds like y in English, e.g., llama is pronounced as yama.

- The letter ñ sounds like ny in English, e.g., año is pronounced as anyo.
- The letter r is rolled or trilled, e.g., Perro is pronounced as per.
- The letter z sounds like s in English, e.g., Zapato is pronounced sapato.

Quechua Phrases

Quechua is the indigenous language of the Incas and their descendants, who still reside in various regions of Peru, notably in the Andean region. It is also one of the official languages of Peru, along with Spanish and other local languages. Quechua has several dialects and variances, depending on the locality and the community. The dialect spoken in the Cusco area, where Machu Picchu is situated, is called Cusco Quechua or Southern Quechua. Here are some popular Quechua words that you may meet or use during your vacation to Machu Picchu: Allillanchu/Allillanmi - Hello/Hello (response)

- Sumaq Punchay - Good day
- Sumaq tuta - Good night
- Imaynalla kashanki? - How are you?

- Allillanmi kashani - I am fine
- Sutiyki? - What is your name?
- Sutiyqa ... - My name is ...
- Maymantam kanki? - Where are you from?
- Noqaykuqa ... suyumanta kanchik - We come from ...
- Rimaykullayki - Nice to meet you
- Añay - Thank you.
- Ama hina kaychu - Please
- Pampachaykuway - Excuse me
- Manan yachakuni - I don't know
- Manan rimani - I don't speak
- Yachakuykuyman - Help me
- Munayni ... - I adore ...

Qusqu llaqtapi Machu Picchuta rikunaykipaqmi hamusqayki? - Have you gone to Cusco to view Machu Picchu?

Arí, Machu Picchuta rikunaykipaqmi hamusqani - Yes, I have come to visit Machu Picchu

Manan, Machu Picchuta rikunaykipaqlla hamusqani, huk pachapim hamusqani - No, I have not come to visit Machu Picchu; I have come for another reason

Machu Picchu sumaq llaqtam Kashan: Machu Picchu is a wonderful site.

Machu Picchupi hayk'asqayku? - How do we travel to Machu Picchu?

Machu Picchupi hayk'anapaqqa, trenwanmi rinayki, icha mikhuwanmi rinayki, icha salkantay trekwanmi rinayki - To go to Machu Picchu, you may travel by train, or by bus, or by the Salkantay trek

Some recommendations on how to pronounce Quechua words are:

The letter q sounds like k in English, but with more aspiration, e.g., qusqu is pronounced as khus-khu.

The letter h sounds like a delicate breath, e.g., hayk'a is pronounced as hai-kha.

The letter k sounds like a hard c in English, e.g., kanchik is pronounced as kan-chik.

The letter y sounds like ee in English, e.g., yachakuni is pronounced as ee-a-chakuni.

The letter ch sounds like ch in English, e.g., ch'arki is pronounced char-ki.

Learning some simple words in Spanish and Quechua will increase your experience and comprehension of Machu Picchu and its culture. You may use these words to connect with locals, guides, and other tourists and demonstrate respect and admiration for the people and the location. You may discover more about the history, customs, and beliefs of the Incas and their descendants, who have retained their language and identity for centuries. By uttering certain words in their languages, you may connect with them and their history in a deeper and more meaningful manner.

CONCLUSION

You have concluded our Machu Picchu travel guide, and we hope you have enjoyed reading it. Machu Picchu is a destination that will remain with you forever, making you feel alive and linked with nature, history, and culture. Whether you visit it by rail, bus, or walking, you will be surprised by its beauty and mystery, and you will learn a lot about the Inca civilization and its legacy.

This book has supplied you with all the information you need to plan your journey to Machu Picchu, from how to purchase your admission ticket to what to see and do to how to behave and respect the site. We have also given you some ideas on how to make the most of your stay, avoid typical traps, and have a safe and pleasurable trip. We have attempted to be as accurate and up-to-date as possible, but please remember that things may change due to weather, restrictions, or other causes. Always check the official websites or agencies before buying your ticket or excursion.

We hope this guide has motivated you to visit Machu Picchu or revisit it if you have previously been there. Machu Picchu is a site that demands your attention and appreciation, a place that will improve your life and your trips. We wish you a safe voyage to Machu Picchu.

Printed in Great Britain
by Amazon